Collins · FLAGSHIP HISTORYMAKERS

Series Editor: Derrick Murphy

MUSSOLINI

Collins · FLAGSHIP HISTORYMAKERS

MUSSOLINI

DERRICK MURPHY

Collins

An imprint of HarperCollins*Publishers*

William Collins' dream of knowledge for all began with the publication of his first book in 1819. A self-educated mill worker, he not only enriched millions of lives, but also founded a flourishing publishing house. Today, staying true to this spirit, Collins books are packed with inspiration, innovation and practical expertise. They place you at the centre of a world of possibility and give you exactly what you need to explore it.

Collins. Do more.

Published by Collins
An imprint of HarperCollins*Publishers*
77–85 Fulham Palace Road
Hammersmith
London
W6 8JB

You might also like to visit
www.harpercollins.co.uk
The book lovers' website

Browse the complete Collins catalogue at
www.collinseducation.com

© HarperCollins*Publishers* Ltd 2005

10 9 8 7 6 5 4 3 2 1

ISBN 0 00 719917 1

British Library Cataloguing in Publication Data
A Catalogue record for this publication is available from the British Library

Series commissioned by Graham Bradbury
Project management and edited by Marie Insall
Book design by Derek Lee
Map artwork by Richard Morris
Picture research by Celia Dearing
Production by Sarah Robinson
Printed and bound by Printing Express, Hong Kong

ACKNOWLEDGEMENTS

The publishers would like to thank the following for permission to reproduce extracts from their books:

IPC+Syndication for the extract from *Mussolini, The Study of Demagogue* by Sir Ivone Kirkpatrick (Odhams Press, 1964). Weidenfeld & Nicolson for the extract from *Mussolini* by Denis Mack Smith (1981).

The Publishers would like to thank the following for permission to reproduce pictures on these pages T=Top, B=Bottom, L=Left, R=Right, C=Centre

akg-images, London 12, 15T, 24B, 49, 57, 58, akg-images, London/Ullstein 32, 33; © Corbis/Underwood & Underwood 14T, © Corbis/Bettmann 14B, 27, 35, 42, 56, © Corbis/Hulton-Deutsch Collection 21; © Getty Images/New York Times Co. 9, © Getty Images/Hulton Archive 15B, 19, © Getty Images/Keystone/Hulton Archive 23, © Getty Images/Topical Press Agency/Hulton Archive 24T.

Cover picture: www.bridgeman.co.uk/ Private Collection

Every effort has been made to contact the holders of copyright material, but if any have been inadvertently overlooked the Publishers will be pleased to make the necessary arrangements at the first opportunity.

Contents

Why do historians differ?

THE purpose of the Flagship Historymakers series is to explore the main debates surrounding a number of key individuals in British, European and American History.

Each book begins with a chronology of the significant events in the life of the particular individual, and an outline of the person's career. The book then examines in greater detail three of the most important and controversial issues in the life of the individual – issues which continue to attract differing views from historians, and which feature prominently in examination syllabuses in A-level History and beyond.

Each of these issue sections provides students with an overview of the main argument put forward by historians. By posing key questions, these sections aim to help students to think through the areas of debate and to form their own judgments on the evidence. It is important, therefore, for students to understand why historians differ in their views on past events and, in particular, on the role of individuals in past events.

The study of history is an ongoing debate about events in the past. Although factual evidence is the essential ingredient of history, it is the *interpretation* of factual evidence that forms the basis for historical debate. The study of why historians differ is termed 'historiography'.

Historical debate can occur for a wide variety of reasons.

Insufficient evidence

In some cases there is insufficient evidence to provide a definitive conclusion. In attempting to 'fill the gaps' where factual evidence is unavailable, historians use their professional judgements to make 'informed comments' about the past.

Availability of evidence

It wasn't until the 1960s that material on Mussolini started to become available from the Italian state archives. As a result, historians have had access to historical evidence that was unavailable to historians who studied Mussolini before the 1960s. Also, when historians study Mussolini's foreign policy, it is important that they have access to the state archives of other states that were important in Mussolini's foreign policy.

Other important sources of evidence have been Mussolini's auto-biography and his writings in *Avanti!* and *Il Popolo d'Italia* newspapers, and the memoirs of leading Fascists.

'A philosophy of history?'

Many historians have a specific view of history that will affect the way they make their historical judgements. For instance, Marxist historians – who take the view from the writings of Karl Marx the founder of modern socialism – believe that society has been made up of competing economic and social classes. They also place consider-able importance on economic reasons in human decision making. Therefore, a Marxist historian looking at an historical issue may take a completely different viewpoint to a non-Marxist historian.

The role of the individual

The development of history has produced two distinct and opposing schools of thought. One view emphasises the role of social, economic and political factors in bringing historical change. The other high-lights the role of individuals who by their ideas, personalities and abilities have literally changed the course of history. Such individuals were Hitler, Lenin and Mussolini. Biographers of Mussolini place great emphasis on Mussolini's abilities. However, it could be argued that the social, economic and political conditions created by the trauma of the First World War were more important. Looking at Italian history from this perspective, historians suggest that the impact of the war made the collapse of the Liberal political system and the rise of Fascist-style regimes across Europe inevitable.

Placing different emphasis on the same historical evidence

Even if historians do not possess different philosophies of history or place different emphasis on the role of the individual, it is still possible for them to disagree in one very important way. This is that they may place different emphases on aspects of the same factual evidence. As a result, History should be seen as a subject that encourages debate about the past, based on historical evidence.

Summary

Historical debate is, in its nature, continuous. What today may be an accepted view about a past event may well change in the future, as the debate continues.

Timeline: Mussolini's life

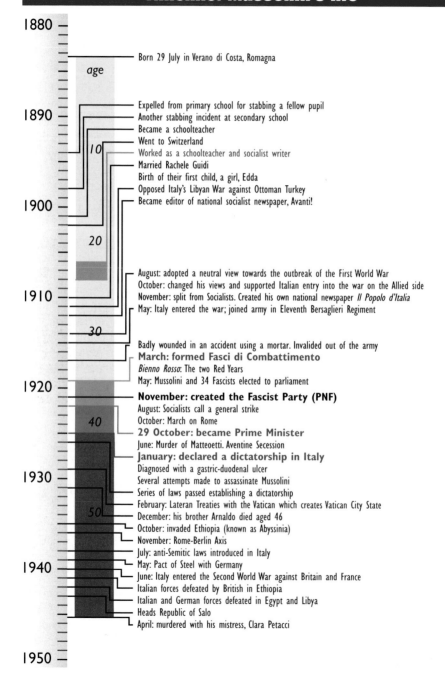

1880

Born 29 July in Verano di Costa, Romagna

age

1890

Expelled from primary school for stabbing a fellow pupil
Another stabbing incident at secondary school
Became a schoolteacher
Went to Switzerland
Worked as a schoolteacher and socialist writer

10

Married Rachele Guidi
Birth of their first child, a girl, Edda
Opposed Italy's Libyan War against Ottoman Turkey
Became editor of national socialist newspaper, Avanti!

1900

20

August: adopted a neutral view towards the outbreak of the First World War
October: changed his views and supported Italian entry into the war on the Allied side
November: split from Socialists. Created his own national newspaper *Il Popolo d'Italia*
May: Italy entered the war; joined army in Eleventh Bersaglieri Regiment

1910

30

Badly wounded in an accident using a mortar. Invalided out of the army
March: formed Fasci di Combattimento
Bienno Rosso: The two Red Years
May: Mussolini and 34 Fascists elected to parliament

1920

November: created the Fascist Party (PNF)
August: Socialists call a general strike
October: March on Rome
29 October: became Prime Minister
June: Murder of Matteoetti. Aventine Secession
January: declared a dictatorship in Italy
Diagnosed with a gastric-duodenal ulcer
Several attempts made to assassinate Mussolini
Series of laws passed establishing a dictatorship
February: Lateran Treaties with the Vatican which creates Vatican City State

40

1930

50

December: his brother Arnaldo died aged 46
October: invaded Ethiopia (known as Abyssinia)
November: Rome-Berlin Axis
July: anti-Semitic laws introduced in Italy
May: Pact of Steel with Germany
June: Italy entered the Second World War against Britain and France
Italian forces defeated by British in Ethiopia
Italian and German forces defeated in Egypt and Libya
Heads Republic of Salo
April: murdered with his mistress, Clara Petacci

1940

1950

Mussolini surrounded by his troops at the height of his dictatorship (1938).

Mussolini: a brief biography

How did Mussolini make history?

In *Mussolini* (1981), British historian Denis Mack Smith states:

'Mussolini was neither born great nor had greatness thrust upon him but had to fight his way out of obscurity by his own ambition and talents.'

Through his own talents, Mussolini rose to become Italy's youngest and longest-serving Prime Minister of the twentieth century. The phrase 'Mussolini's Italy' aptly describes Italian history from 1922 to 1943. As *Il Duce* ('The Leader') Mussolini claimed to personify the Italian spirit. He saw himself as one of history's 'Great Men' whose destiny it was to make Italy 'feared and respected' throughout Europe. As a man of destiny, he saw himself as a latter-day Caesar, re-creating a twentieth-century version of the Roman Empire.

Il Duce: the Italian for 'leader', which Mussolini used to define his position as Prime Minister and leader of Fascism.

Fascism – the beliefs and political system of Mussolini – was used as a model for the creation of similar movements outside of Italy. Fascist-style regimes emerged across not only Europe, but also Latin America. Perhaps the most interesting and controversial impact that Mussolini made outside of Italy was fascism's influence on the Nazi movement in Germany.

Although Mussolini died a political failure in April 1945, Fascism lived on. Today, supporters of authoritarian, anti-liberal, nationalist movements are termed neo-Fascist.

Upbringing, education and marriage

Mussolini was born on Sunday 29 July 1883, in the small hamlet of Verano di Costa in the parish of Predappio, in the Romagna region of central Italy. His father, Alessandro, was a blacksmith who had strong socialist political views. His mother, Rosa, had been a schoolteacher and was a devout Roman Catholic. He was baptised Benito Amilcare Andrea Mussolini: Benito, after the Mexican revolutionary of the 1860s, Benito Juarez; Amilcare, after Amilcare Capriani, a follower of Garibaldi, who also fought for the Paris Commune in 1871; and Andrea, from Andrea Costa, an Italian revolutionary who led an uprising against the Italian government in Bologna, capital of the Romagna, in 1874. Mussolini was the eldest of three children. Arnaldo was born on 11 January 1885 and was an important influence on Mussolini in later life. Edvige, a girl, was born in 1888.

From his father, Mussolini inherited a support for socialism and a dislike of clerical involvement in politics. However, his mother ensured that he was brought up within the Roman Catholic Church. Mussolini has been portrayed as a wayward youngster with a tendency towards violence and bullying. At the age of 11, at the **Salesian** College, Faenza, he was expelled for stabbing a fellow pupil in the hand with a knife. In 1894 at a state school in Forlimpopoli, he was accused of stabbing another pupil, this time in the buttocks. Mussolini is thought to have excelled in language, literature and teaching, while stuggling in mathematics and agriculture. He developed a lifelong interest in music, and in his later life was proficient in both French and German.

Salesian: order of Catholic Priests engaged in education.

Following his formal education, Mussolini spent time teaching and travelling. In Switzerland, from 1902 to 1904, he worked in manual jobs where he met fellow socialists. More importantly, he began writing for socialist newspapers and developed a reputation as a competent journalist.

In 1900, Mussolini met his future wife, Rachele Guidi, for the first time, in Perdappio. In 1908, they met again in nearby Forli. However, it wasn't until 1910 that they eventually married, when it was clear that Rachele was expecting their first child. They had five children: Edda (b. 1910); Vittorio (b. 1916); Bruno (b. 1918); Romano (b. 1927); and Anna Maria (b. 1929). Even though Mussolini had a succession of mistresses throughout his life, and fathered at least one illegitimate child, they stayed married for the next 35 years until Mussolini's death. Rachele died on 31 October 1979 in Forli.

A leading socialist

From 1906 to 1914, Mussolini developed a reputation as a journalist for socialist newspapers. In January 1910, back in the Romagna, he started his own local socialist newspaper called *La Lotta di Classe* ('The Class Struggle'). Through his journalism, Mussolini began to develop a nationally recognised reputation in socialist circles. A turning point came on 7 July 1912 when Mussolini spoke at the national Socialist Party Congress in Reggio, Emilia. He demanded revolutionary action and the expulsion of right-wing Socialist moderates from the party. His views were supported by the congress. In November 1912, he was appointed editor of the national socialist paper, *Avanti!* ('Forward'). Mussolini seemed to be heading towards a national career as a leading Socialist.

The First World War: the turning point in his career

The outbreak of the First World War in August 1914 transformed Mussolini's career. Italy initially remained neutral, supported by the Italian Socialist Party (PSI). However, on 18 October, Mussolini wrote an article in *Avanti!* that changed his life. Entitled 'From absolute neutrality to an active working neutrality', he advocated Italian entry into the war on the Allied side. As a result, he was expelled from the PSI on 24 November.

Mussolini's sudden change of view can be attributed to a number of factors. First, was the almost universal acceptance of the World War by other European socialist parties, most notably the German Social Democrats. Secondly, he was affected by his failure to gain election to parliament as a Socialist in the 1913 election. Finally, the failure of a national general strike called 'Red Week' in June 1914 may have convinced him that socialism was weak in Italy. After his expulsion, he set up his own national paper, *Il Popolo D'Italia* ('The Italian People'), which supported Italian participation in the war.

In May 1915, Italy entered the war. Mussolini was called up for military service and later, in 1917, he suffered serious injuries in an accident involving a mortar. He was invalided from the army with the rank of corporal. It was also a momentous year for Italy. In October the army suffered a major defeat at Caporetto by Austro-German forces. By the end of the war Italy had been transformed: millions had served in the army; over 600 000 were killed; the economy was gravely weakened through inflation and war production; and the Peace Treaties of 1919/20 failed to provide Italy with the territory that she had fought the war to gain. The occupation of Fiume by **Gabriele D'Annunzio** highlighted the weakness of the Italian government. The immediate post-war period (1918–21) was characterised by economic crisis, social unrest and national humiliation. The introduction of universal **suffrage** transformed the political situation in Italy. Until 1919 Italy had been governed by a narrow, middle class liberal elite.

Suffrage: the right to vote.

Gabriele D'Annunzio (1863–1938)
A nationalist writer and noted soldier in the First World War. He received medals for bravery and even flew over Vienna in August 1918, dropping propaganda leaflets. He was appalled by the terms of the Peace Treaties at the end of the war. In particular, he thought that Italy should have received the Adriatic port of Fiume, which was given to the new state of Yugoslavia. However, he occupied the port in September 1919, creating a city-state with policies similar to what became Fascism. He was forced out of Fiume by Italian armed forces in 1920.

Understanding Mussolini

- Up until Italy's entry into the First World War he was **a fervent socialist**. From 1925 he created a right-wing dictatorship, which aimed to destroy Italian socialism.

- As the editor of *Avanti!* and *Il Popolo d'Italia* newspapers he was **a nationally known journalist**. As dictator of Italy, he greatly limited the power of the press.

- He was a politician who tried to give the appearance of **a European statesman**, but he was always willing to use either violence or the threat of violence to gain his political ends.

- **He claimed to have created a totalitarian state after 1925**. However, both the Roman Catholic Church and the monarchy survived his dictatorship.

- As dictator of Italy he **supported the monarchy and opposed socialism**. As ruler of the Salo Republic he supported anti-monarchist and socialist-style policies.

- **A devoted family man**; he loved his children but was constantly unfaithful to his wife and had a series of mistresses.

- He portrayed **a public image of health and vigour** as *Il Duce*. Privately, he was a sick man who suffered from stomach ulcers.

- He claimed that **Italian Fascism was not for export** but spent much of his time in power supporting Fascist-style groups in Spain, Austria and Croatia.

- He **aimed for Italy to be a great European power** with a large colonial empire. However, he led Italy into the Second World War on Germany's side, which led to the collapse of his regime.

- He was **the longest-serving Prime Minister of Italy** in the twentieth century but was murdered by fellow Italians.

> '*Mussolini, though it was he who first announced the intention of building 'a totalitarian state', was but a Sawdust Ceasar, not more than a buffoon.*'
> Prof. R. J. B. Bosworth (Mussolini, 2002)

**Victor Emmanuel III
(1869–1947)**
King of Italy from 1900 to 1946. Against the wishes of parliament, he took Italy into the First World War on the Allied side (1915), and appointed Mussolini as Prime Minister (1922). Mussolini made him Emperor of Abyssina (1936) and King of Albania (1939). He dismissed Mussolini when the Allied success in the Second World War became obvious (1943). He abdicated in 1946 and died in exile in Egypt.

Acerbo Law: a new electoral law which aimed to transform Fascism's minority status by proposing that any party gaining more votes than any of its rivals, providing that it gained at least 25 per cent of the total, would be entitled to two-thirds of the seats in the assembly.

From 1919 two new mass political parties emerged, the Socialist Party (PSI) and the Catholic Party (PPI).

Italy's youngest Prime Minister

At the end of October 1922 the King, **Victor Emmanuel III**, invited Mussolini to become Prime Minister of a right-wing coalition government. At the age of 39 he was the youngest ever Prime Minister. He was able to achieve this position by exploiting the social, economic and political crises that affected post-war Italy. In March 1919, he created the *Fasci di Combattimento* ('Combat Group'), which was anti-socialist, anti-liberal and nationalist. From 1919 to 1922 it became a major force in Italian politics. Mussolini was able to play on the fear of socialism to gain support from big business, landowners and members of the liberal elite. Using a mixture of legitimate political activity through parliament, and the threat of violence, Mussolini was in a position by October 1922 to make a play for political power.

Mussolini was chosen as Prime Minister for two reasons. First, the King feared that if he opposed the Fascists a civil war would ensue. Secondly, Liberal politicians such as **Giovanni Giolitti** thought that they could control Mussolini for their own purposes.

In the end, Mussolini was chosen in an attempt to end the political chaos. As the head of a coalition government in which the Fascists were a minority, it was hoped that Mussolini would abandon the use of violence.

The Fascist dictator

From October 1922 to January 1925, Mussolini was able to create a dictatorship. This was partly due to the split in the Italian left wing between the Socialist Party (PSI) and Communist Party (PCI), which had occurred in 1921. Also, the Liberal politicians were split into rival factions. Ultimately, Mussolini depended on the support of the King. In addition, Pope Pius XI gave tacit support to Mussolini as the only real alternative to socialism. The passing of the **Acerbo Law** in 1923 altered the electoral law, which enabled Mussolini to

**Giovanni Giolitti
(1842–1928)**
Liberal Prime Minister of Italy: 1901–3; 1906–19; 1911–14; 1920/1. He was a supporter of 'transformism', the idea that governments should be created that reflect a broad section of political opinion. He believed that the Fascists could become part of a broad national-conservative coalition. However, he completely underestimated Mussolini.

Giacomo Matteotti (1885–1924)
A Socialist deputy for the PSI who was first elected to government in 1919. From a wealthy family, he graduated in Law from the University of Bologna. He distinguished himself as one of the most persitent and determined opponents of the Fascists. In his speech in parliament on 30 May 1924 he denounced Fascism. On 10 June he was kidnapped on his way to parliament, severly beaten and then killed by Fascist thugs.

gain a massive Fascist victory in the 1924 elections. He also merged the Fascists with the Nationalists. However, the turning point in the creation of a dictatorship came with the murder of Socialist deputy **Giacomo Matteotti** in June 1924 by Fascist thugs. Socialists and Liberals played into Mussolini's hands by withdrawing from parliament in protest. With the support of the King, army and business elite Mussolini survived the Matteotti crisis.

In January 1925, Mussolini declared his dictatorship and claimed that he had created a totalitarian regime. Yet compared to the other inter-war dictators, such as Hitler and Stalin, he was the least dictatorial. A secret police (OVRA) was created, and the Fascists used violence against their opponents. However, the powerful Roman Catholic Church, the monarchy and the army remained outside of his control. As R. J. B. Bosworth in *Mussolini* (2002) states: 'Mussolini's image is of the dictator with limited ability to dictate.'

Despite this, Mussolini gave the impression of a dynamic leader: he liked fast cars, horse riding and flying; he enjoyed showing off his athleticism by appearing in public bare-chested and jogging in military uniform. However, from 1925 he was diagnosed with a gastro-duodenal ulcer which forced him to follow a strict diet of milk and fruit. Thus, the portrayed image was very different from the actual reality.

Creation of a new Roman Empire?

Mussolini's greatest aim was to make Italy 'feared and respected' in the world. He aimed to create a large colonial empire in East Africa. To achieve this he conquered Ethiopia (Abyssinia) from October 1935. He also had plans to acquire the Sudan, which was administered by Britain. During Mussolini's rule, Italy gained Jubaland from British East Africa in 1925, Ethiopia in 1935/6 and Albania in 1939. However, in doing so Mussolini alienated himself from Britain and France, and helped to force Italy into a fatal friendship with **Adolf Hitler**.

Adolf Hitler (1889–1945)
The Austrian-born dictator of Germany. He became leader of the Nazi Party in 1920 and German Chancellor in 1933. Hitler created the extreme right-wing political ideology of Nazism, which included the principles of Aryan superiority, the Germans being considered as the 'master race'; a policy of anti-communism; anti-Semitism and racism; the building up of the armed forces; and a determination to regain lost territory.

Brutal friendship with Hitler

**Spanish Civil War
(1936–9)**: a war
between a socialist-
communist government
(Republicans) and the Army
and Conservatives
(Nationalists), led by
General Franco. Mussolini
supported the Nationalists.

**Rome-Berlin Axis
(1936)**: an agreement of
cooperation between Italy
and Germany in November
1936.

**Anti-Comintern
Pact (1937)**: an
extension of the Rome-
Berlin Axis to include
Japan. The title of the pact
suggested that it was anti-
communist.

**Pact of Steel
(1939)**: an alliance
between Italy and
Germany, which increased
Mussolini's links with
Hitler.

**Fascist Grand
Council**: from 1923, it
was the highest political
body in the Italian state
and was given formal legal
status in 1928. As head of
government, Mussolini was
president of the Grand
Council and chose its
membership. The council
last met on 24 July 1943.
At 2:30 a.m. on 25 July, it
declared by majority vote
that the King should
regain his role as
Commander-in-Chief of the
armed forces, from
Mussolini. This led to
Mussolini's dismissal as
Prime Minister by the King
on 25 July.

Initially, Mussolini feared Hitler's designs on Austria and in 1934 opposed the Nazi attempt to gain control there. However, from 1935, Mussolini and Hitler became close allies because they both wanted to change the post-First World War political settlement. This began with their military intervention in the **Spanish Civil War** on the side of Franco and the Nationalists. Then in 1936, the two powers signed the **Rome-Berlin Axis**. The following year they signed the **Anti-Comintern Pact** with Japan, which was concluded in May 1939 by the **Pact of Steel**. However, when Germany went to war with both Britain and France in September 1939, Mussolini remained neutral. He waited until June 1940 – at a point when he believed that Germany had won – to enter the war. This proved to be a terrible mistake.

Italy was completely unprepared for war. From June 1940 to July 1943, Italian forces were defeated by Britain in North Africa and Ethiopia. Italian forces were also defeated by Greece in the winter of 1940/1, and victory was only secured through the intervention of Germany. In July 1943, Sicily was also invaded and occupied by Anglo-American forces.

Mussolini was deposed by the **Fascist Grand Council**, and on 25 July he was dismissed as Prime Minister by the King and arrested. His political career was briefly resurrected when he was released by German paratroops.

The Salo Republic

From September 1943 to his death in April 1945, Mussolini ruled northern Italy as a puppet ruler of the Germans. He created the Social Republic of Salo, although his political influence there was minimal. Mussolini retracted his support for the monarchy and those who had ousted him in July 1943. On 28 April 1945, while fleeing from advancing Anglo-American troops, Mussolini was captured near Lake Como by Italian partisans. The ultimate indignity for Mussolini was to be hung upside down with his mistress, Clara Petacci, in the main square of Milan, the city in which the *Fasci di Combattimento* had been formed in March 1919.

1 ◢ How did he become dictator of Italy?

Did he rise to power because of the weakness of the Liberal political system?

How did he consolidate his hold on power from 1922 to 1925?

Was he merely an opportunist in his rise to power?

Framework of Events

1919	March: Mussolini founded *Fasci di Combattimento* ('Combat Group')
	2–3 November: Fascists heavily defeated in national elections
1919–20	*Bienno Rosso* ('The Two Red Years') created industrial unrest in north Italy
1920	Breakthrough for Fascists with rise of agrarian fascism
1921	Fascists win 35 seats in national elections
	November: Fascist Party (PNF) created
1922	February: Facta became Italian Prime Minister
	Pope Pius XI elected
	August: Failure of general strike broken by Fascists
	27–8 October: Fascist March on Rome
	29 October: Mussolini offered post of Prime Minister
	16 November: Mussolini given extraordinary powers by parliament
	December: Creation of National Fascist Militia (MSVN)
1923	November: Acerbo Election Law passed
1924	April: Fascists win landslide victory in national elections
	June: Murder of Socialist deputy, Matteotti, by Fascist thugs
	Aventine Secession
1925	January: Mussolini declared his dictatorship

O N October 29 1922, King Victor Emmanuel III offered Mussolini the post of Prime Minister. Borrowing a frock coat, Mussolini looked just like his liberal predecessors. However, his rise to political power was both swift and remarkable. Having acquired this power, Mussolini was determined not to give it up. As a result he became both the youngest and longest-serving Italian Prime Minister of the twentieth century. How was this achieved? Was it deep-rooted problems in Italy's political system, brought to the fore by the social, economic and political crises of the First World War, that led to Mussolini's rise to power? Or, was Mussolini, through his own abilities and the support of a few figures, able to gain control of Italy and force it along a completely new political path?

Did Mussolini rise to power because of the weakness of the Liberal political system?

Italy's constitution at the time of Mussolini's rise to power was based upon the limited model that had been granted at the time of Italy's unification in 1861. Italy was a constitutional monarchy, with King Victor Emannuel III recognised as Head of State, which gave him extensive powers. The government, which comprised two chambers, was chosen by the national parliament. Of the two chambers, the King nominated the senate's members, while the Chamber of Deputies was elected. However, the proportion of Italians engaged in national politics was very small. Before 1912, approximately 2.2 per cent of the population had the right to vote. This later rose to 8.6 million, or 24 per cent of the adult population, when the vote was then extended to all male literates over 21 years, or illiterates who had completed over 30 years of military service. Rome's incorporation into the Kingdom of Italy caused Pope Pius IX to lose his own independent territory, which led him to instruct Catholics not to participate in Italian politics. Since the vast majority of Italians were Catholics, this had a profound effect on the political system. The political nation really comprised only a small elite of middle-class politicians who shared political power with the King.

'Transformism': the practice of welding together large and unlikely coalitions in support of ministaries. By granting favours to individuals or to the communities that they represented, ministers might 'transform' opponents into supporters and improve the prospects of their administration and of their legislative programmes.

By 1892, Italy had experienced 28 governments in its 32 years as a unified state. Liberal politicians practiced **'transformism'** in order to ensure political stability. However, rather than involving a wide cross-section of political opinion in government, it merely highlighted the rivalry between senior Liberal politicians. It is easy to see, therefore, how the Italian population viewed the Liberal political system as corrupt.

The Italian political system was further weakened when on 24 May 1915 Prime Minister **Antonio Salandra**, with the support of the King, entered Italy into the First World War on the side of the Allies

Antonio Salandra (1853–1931) Prime Minister from March 1914 to June 1916, he was the chief architect of Italy's entry into the First World War. He was a lawyer and right-wing Liberal, and a deputy from 1886 to 1928. He attempted to create a Liberal-Nationalist coalition during Facta's premiership, and to form a coalition government on 27–28 October, which would include the Fascists. He cooperated with the Fascists until Mussolini's speech of 3 January 1925, announcing a dictatorship.

without consulting either parliament or the Italian people. British historian, Denis Mack Smith, in *Italy: A Modern History* (1967), concludes that Mussolini's Fascism was a political system that naturally developed from a system that had failed to involve the Italian population.

The impact of the First World War

Italy's involvement in the First World War had an immense impact: 600 000 soldiers died; over 400 000 were captured; and three million served in the armed forces. Two battles were of great significance to Italy: Caporetto and Vittorio Veneto. In October 1917, the Italians suffered a major defeat by Austro-German forces at Caporetto, which almost forced Italy out of the war. However, Caporetto resulted in major changes in government and the army, and created a national mood of patriotism. In September 1918, at Vittorio Veneto, Italy won a major victory against the Austro-Hungarian army. It gave Italians the belief that they would be a major beneficiary of the peace treaties after the war. Unfortunately, while they had hoped for large parts of the Dalmatian coast, including the port of Fiume, at the **Paris Peace Conference** Italy received only the Trentino and Trieste. The Peace Treaties were seen as a humiliation for Italy, creating the idea of a 'mutilated victory'.

Paris Peace Conference (1919–20): The assembly held after the First World War during which the League of Nations was set up and the peace agreements between the Allied and Central Powers were worked out. These proceedings were dominated by Britain, France, Italy, Japan and the USA, although 32 nations took part.

The war also placed a great strain on the Italian economy. The cost of living rose 300 per cent, and at the end of the war two million servicemen were demobilised, creating a major unemployment problem. By November 1918, millions of Italians had been involved in a national struggle like never before.

In 1919, a new electoral law created universal suffrage. For the first time the Italian masses had the opportunity to participate in national politics. Also in 1919, Pope Benedict XV (1914–22) allowed the creation of the Catholic Political Party (the Popolari or PPI). Thus from 1919, Italy entered the realm of mass politics. The old liberal elite found it very difficult to adjust. In the November 1919

Landmark Study The book that changed people's views

F. L. Carsten, *The Rise of Fascism* (B.T. Batsford Ltd., 1967)

This study provided one of the first comprehensive studies behind the rise of Fascist-style regimes across Europe in the inter-war period. Carsten was able to provide parallels between the rise of Fascism in Italy with other states, most notably Germany, but also Fascist movements in states such as Austria. To Carsten, the First World War was the defining event in the rise of Fascism, radicalising politics in Italy. Millions had been directly affected by the war either in the armed forces or by the social and economic impact of the war. However, Carsten linked this development with the weakness of the Italian political system. He argued that the war provided the conditions for the collapse of that system. Finally, he emphasised the role of the threat of socialism and communism as an important factor in rallying support behind the Fascists. Fascist success was aided by the split in the left between PSI and Communists from the beginning of 1921. After the split the two left-wing groups fought each other as much as challenging the Fascists.

elections they faced the new challenge of the PSI and PPI. Both parties did exceptionally well at the expense of the Liberals.

In *The Rise of Fascism* (1967), historian F. L. Carsten claims that Fascism did not exist before the First World War but rather it was this great social, economic and political upheaval that created the conditions for it to arise. Mussolini was able to exploit these conditions to gain political power.

Was Mussolini merely an opportunist in his rise to power?

Historians Denis Mack Smith and Renzo de Felice regard Mussolini's personality as being central in his rise to power. He is viewed as an opportunist, exploiting situations and reacting to circumstances in order to gain power.

In March 1919, Mussolini had founded the *Fasci di Combattimento*, whose programme was anti-clerical, anti-monarchist, nationalist and in favour of social reform. However, at this time, Italy was suffering from a severe post-war social and economic crisis, which successive Italian governments seemed incapable of dealing with. In 1919, unemployment reached two million. The wholesale price index that had been 100 in 1913 had risen to 412.9 by the end of the war in 1918, and to 590.7 by 1920. The value of shares halved in the same period. The **lira** fell from 30 to the pound in March 1919, to 100 to the pound by December 1920. Membership of socialist trade unions rose from 250 000 in 1918, to 1.2 million by 1920. This resulted in two years of social unrest (1919/20), which were associated with trade union strikes and civil unrest. This period was termed *Bienno Rosso* ('Two Red Years').

Lira: the italian currency prior to the introduction of the Euro in January 2001.

Mussolini assumes a characteristic pose as he speaks to an audience in Italy in 1934.

Mussolini exploited the failure of successive Italian governments to deal with the post-war crisis. An example of this was Gabriele D'Annunzio's occupation of Fiume in September 1919. War hero D'Annunzio managed to achieve something that the Italian government had failed to do in 1918: acquire territory promised to Italy by the **Treaty of London**, and which they failed to receive at the Paris Peace Conference, creating their 'mutilated victory'. For 14 months D'Annunzio created a corporate state. He had his supporters dressed in black shirts and used the traditional Roman salute. Only after considerable international pressure did the Italian government send troops to expel D'Annunzio. In *Modern Italy* (1984), historian Martin Clark states that 'D'Annunzio had proven that the Italian state was weak, that the army could be disloyal and had pioneered a new style of mass politics'. Mussolini quickly had his Fascist *Squadristi* ('Squad') adopt the traditional Roman salute and dress in black shirts, capitalising on D'Annunzio's achievement.

Treaty of London (1915): a treaty between the Allies and Italy. It promised Italy territory from Austria-Hungary, including the Trentino and Trieste. It also promised the modern-day coastline of Slovenia and Croatia, known as Dalmatia.

Fascist policy, however, was unpopular, and in the elections of November 1919 they failed to win any seats. Although the PSI won 156 seats, while the newly formed PPI won 107, it proved to be a disaster for all government parties. Mussolini reacted by simply changing the party programme.

Indeed the fragmented nature of the Fascist movement in 1919/20 actually helped Mussolini in his quest for power. Fascist

Ras: Ethiopian term for local chieftain, which was used to describe local bosses of Fascist movements.

groups with a range of political opinions, from radical to conservative, started to appear spontaneously across industrial areas in northern and central Italy. Fascist *Ras* leaders of these groups possessed considerable political power. Mussolini managed to hold this disparate movement together by keeping the party programme flexible, and altering policy to suit specific situations. His newspaper, *Il Popolo d'Italia*, became a great tool through which to get his views to the Italian public. He was also an exceptional public speaker and a nationally known figure, all of which he exploited.

The climax of *Bienno Rosso* came in August 1920 with the occupation of factories by socialist trade unionists across northern Italy. At this time, however, the Fascist movement also had a breakthrough as it began to develop support in rural areas. By 1920, *Federterra* ('socialist peasant leagues') had arisen, which led to the growth of anti-socialist sentiment in both urban and rural areas of Italy, which the Fascists exploited. Mussolini, therefore, changed the party policy, adopting a more conservative, nationalist and anti-socialist programme, which provided a more attractive alternative to the social and political chaos facing Italy. A mixture of legitimate political activity and illegal violence against political opponents enabled him to implement these changes. Mussolini's Fascist *Squadristi* terrorised opponents by attacking trade union halls and the offices of the PSI and *Avanti!*. Arson and murder were the hallmarks of Fascist violence and this 'twin track' approach of legal and illegal methods was a consistent feature of Mussolini's method of operation, even after he acquired political power.

Giovanni Giolitti's government proved incapable of solving the growing social and economic problems, which led him to call a general election in May 1921. Giolitti had hoped to see a major fall in PSI support. However, the PSI still managed to return 122 deputies. With the PPI's refusal to serve under Giolitti, a new Prime Minister, Francesco Nitti, took office. This election was important for Mussolini. The Fascists received seven per cent of the vote, acquiring 35 seats, including one for Mussolini. As a deputy, Mussolini could no longer be arrested for any association with violence. This was particularly crucial for a court case in which he was claimed to have planned to violently overthrow the government. To give his government a broader base, Giolitti had hoped to include the Fascists – Mussolini refused. From 1921 to October 1922, successive Liberal politicians attempted to co-opt the support of Mussolini, which gave the Fascists obvious respectability. Mussolini's skill in this situation was in refusing to accept any post other than Prime Minister.

Italian Prime Ministers in office

Paolo Boselli	June 1916 – Oct. 1917	1 years 4 months
Vittorio Orlando	Oct. 1917 – June 1919	1 year 7 months
Francesco Nitti	June 1919 – June 1920	1 year
Giovanni Giolitti	June 1920 – July 1921	1 year 1 month
Ivanoe Bonomi	July 1921 – Feb. 1922	7 months
Luigi Facta	Feb. 1922 – Oct. 1922	8 months
Benito Mussolini	Oct. 1922 – July 1943	20 years 9 months

In August 1921, Mussolini signed a pact of pacification with the PSI to bring mutual attacks of violence to an end, which caused a temporary crisis within the Fascist movement. Three of the most important local *Ras*, Dino Grandi, Italo Balbo and **Roberto Farinacci**, refused to accept it. In an attempt to outflank his *Ras* opponents, Mussolini resigned briefly as *Il Duce*. He correctly calculated that without his national leadership, the movement would fragment. At a congress of urban Fascists, later in August, Mussolini admitted that he made a mistake in signing the pact, and through his great oratorical skill he won back the support of the rank and file, and the leadership. The congress marked the final transformation of the Fascists into a movement that was clearly anti-socialist and in favour of free enterprise capitalism.

Indeed, by 1921, Fascism had firmly established itself across northern and central Italy. On 9 November, Mussolini took the step of uniting these disparate Fascist movements as the Fascist Party (PNF). His reputation and charisma enabled him to transform Fascism from a nationalist alternative to socialism, into a nationalist, anti-socialist defender of Italy's law and order. Liberal politicians such as Giolitti believed that Fascist violence was merely a sign of the times rather than a permanent characteristic of the

Roberto Farinacci (1892–1945)
A *Ras* of Cremona, he was one of the original Fascists from the meeting in Milan on March 23 1919. In the summer of 1922 he was appointed Consul General of the Fascist militia. From 1925/6 he was secretary to the PNF and was responsible for limiting the power of the press and the 'fascistisation' of the civil service. He was a member of the Fascist Grand Council from 1933, and fought in the Ethiopian War in the air force. He led the anti-Semitic campaign from 1938 against the Jews, and was executed by Italian partisans on 28 April 1945.

**Luigi Facta
(1861–1930)**
Prime Minister from February to October 1922, deputy from 1892 to 1924, and lawyer by profession, he served as a minister in several governments from 1903. His government failed to contain rising political violence between Fascists and Socialists.

party programme. However, Fascist acts of violence enabled Mussolini to ensure that Italy remained ungovernable. He continued to support violence against political opponents while promoting Fascism as a national movement that could bring order to Italy. Denis Mack Smith, in *Mussolini* (1981), claims that: 'Fascism was not a system of immutable (unchanging) beliefs but a path to power'. When Mussolini's policies didn't gain him power, he simply changed them.

Pyschological warfare: The March on Rome

The appointment of **Luigi Facta** as Prime Minister in February 1922 greatly aided Mussolini in his quest for power. Denis Mack Smith describes Facta as 'a negligible politician' who was chosen because the other major Liberal politicians (Giolitti, Salandra and Orlando) were too jealous of each other. As the last Liberal Prime Minister of Italy, Facta seemed incapable of dealing with political violence between Fascists and Socialists. A contemporary comment on the Prime Minister was that he should be called 'verba' not 'facta' because he talked (verba) and never acted (facta).

In February, at the time of the general election, the Alliance of Labour was created from the socialist trade unions. In August, it organised a 24-hour general strike, which the Fascists helped to break up through violence. The Facta government was unable to deal with the situation.

Mussolini leading the March on Rome on 28 October 1922.

Mussolini used the psychological threat of violence and civil war to win power. On 24 October, a mass meeting of Fascists was held in Naples. Mussolini declared that 'either they let us govern or we will seize power by marching on Rome'. By the night of 27 October, Fascists were gathering at four points around Rome (Perugia, Civita Vecchia, Monterotondo and Tivoli) ready to march on the capital. On the night of 27 to 28 October, Fascist squads occupied telephone exchanges and government offices across northern Italy. At 2:00 a.m. on the morning of 28 October, Facta acted. He asked for the King to impose martial law and send in the army to stop the Fascists. The King agreed. However, by 9:00 a.m. the King had changed his mind and refused to impose martial law. Facta resigned. The King then called on Salandra to form a coalition government with the Fascists. Mussolini refused and in his newspaper *Il Popolo d'Italia* declared: 'fascism would not abuse its victory. Let that be clear to all. Fascism wants power and will have it.'. On the advice of Giolitti, the King invited Mussolini to be Prime Minister on 29 October.

The role of the King and Liberal politicians

Mussolini became Italian Prime Minister at the head of a broad coalition government of the centre and right of Italian politics. At

Mussolini's First Government, October 1922

Mussolini (Fascist)	Prime Minister, Minister of the Interior, Foreign Minister
General Armando Diaz (Non-Party)	Minister of War
Federzoni (Nationalist)	Minister of Colonies
Oviglio (Fascist)	Minister of Justice
De Stefani (Fascist)	Minister of Finance
Tangorra (PPI)	Minister of Treasury
Gentile (Nationalist)	Minister of Education
Carnazza (Democrat)	Minister of Public Works
D'Araso (Liberal)	Minister of Agriculture
Rossi (Democrat)	Minister of Industry and Commerce
Cavazonni (PPI)	Minister of Labour and Social Welfare
De Cesare (Democrat)	Minister of Posts and Telegraph
Giurati (Fascist)	Minsiter of Liberated Provinces

the critical moment, in October 1922, he had been greatly assisted in his quest for power by the King. Why did the King change his mind about introducing martial law?

In *Mussolini* (1964), historian Sir Ivone Kirkpatrick argues that the King had been visited in the night by generals Diaz and Pecori Giraldi, who had insisted that the army would do its duty under martial law but stressed that he would be 'well not to put it (the army) to the test.' Alan Cassels, in *Fascist Italy* (1982), believes that the King was persuaded by Fascist sympathisers at the Court, and was also threatened with the idea that he might be replaced as King by his brother the Duke D'Aosta, who was a Fascist sympathiser. Denis Mack Smith asserts that Giolitti advised the King to choose Mussolini, a view supported by R. J. B. Bosworth, who claims:

> 'the main politicians eyed each other but could not unite. Salandra, Orlando and Giolitti, each awaited his own return to the Prime Ministership, but each indicated a preference that the post be entrusted to the young Mussolini rather than to a hated old rival.'

Finally, the King, receiving reports of the March on Rome, feared a civil war in which only the socialists or communists would benefit. In this sense he was partly duped. There were fewer than 30 000 Fascist militia, and these were poorly armed and had little food. Where the army had already begun to occupy public buildings, they had received little opposition from Fascists. In the end only 12 people died in the March on Rome, and many of these deaths were due to private vendettas. Mussolini's 'twin track' approach of acting like a legitimate politician while also using violent, non-parliamentary methods had been successful.

How did Mussolini consolidate his hold on power from 1922 to 1925?

Although Mussolini was Italian Prime Minister from October 1922, he still had very limited power. The PNF were a minority in the coalition government with only a small number of seats in the Chamber of Deputies and no representation in the Upper House, the senate. Mussolini could also still be sacked by the King. However, within just over two years Mussolini was confident enough to declare himself dictator.

There were many factors that helped Mussolini to consolidate his hold on power and declare his dictatorship. One factor was the

Fascist Violence: An Example

'These raids were usually done with either the support of the police or with police knowledge. On 23 January 1921, Balbo for the first time led Fascists in the city of Ferrara on a raid into the countryside, and followed it up with similar raids in February and March. They marched into villages with a twenty-mile radius of Ferrara, beating up Socialists, occasionally killing them, and burning socialist newspaper offices, meeting places, and local party headquarters. Sometimes they merely harassed Socialists, shouting obscenities to them in the street and driving close to them on their motor cycles.'

From *Mussolini* by Jasper Ridley, 1997

Pope Pius XI (1922–39)
He was elected the same month as Facta became Prime Minister, February 1922. Born Achille Ratti, he had been Apostolic Visitor to Poland in 1918. He had witnessed, at first hand, the Communist invasion of Poland in the Russo-Polish War. From that moment on he had an acute dislike of communism.

Vatican: the headquarters of the Roman Catholic Church based in Rome.

appointment of **Pope Pius XI**, an overt anti-communist who, unlike his predecessor, felt that Catholics should not be heavily involved in politics. Sir Odo Russell, British Minister to the **Vatican**, outlined how 'Pius XI wished to withdraw the Church as far as possible from politics, so that Catholics may unite on a religious and moral basis.' As a result, the Pope was instrumental in getting the leader of the PPI, a Sicilian priest called Dom Luigi Sturzo, to resign on 10 July 1923, which meant that the Catholic PPI no longer proved a threat to Mussolini and the PNF.

Another factor was Mussolini's skill in acquiring support from the Catholic Church. He ordered religious instruction in all state-run schools and banned obscene publications and the use of contraceptives. Finally, he increased the salaries of priests and bishops, which were paid out of the public purse.

Even after becoming Prime Minister, Mussolini was still aided by the support, real or tacit, of Liberal politicians, which enabled him further to consolidate his power. On 16 November he addressed parliament, requesting extraordinary powers as Prime Minister in order to deal with the political and economic crisis. He advocated a policy that would end political violence, instil national discipline and create a balanced budget. Mussolini was supported in his request by five former Prime Ministers; Nitti alone refused. With only five abstentions, only 26 senators out of 398 voted against Mussolini.

Another important factor was the merger between the PNF and the Nationalists in February 1923. To cement this merger, Mussolini emphasised his role as the national saviour of Italy in foreign affairs.

Lausanne Conference (1923): the final peace settlement between Turkey and the Allies after the Second World War. Turkey surrendered all claim to former territories of the Ottoman Empire occupied by non-Turks. Italy kept the Dodecanese Islands.

League of Nations (1920): an international organisation created after the First World War in order to preserve the peace and settle disputes by discussion and agreement. Based on the idea of collective security, it had limited influence because its only weapon against wayward members was sanctions, and it failed to prevent aggression among member states. The USA never joined and the USSR only joined the League in 1934. Japan, Germany and Italy left the League in the 1930s.

Gerrymander: deliberately altering the boundaries of election districts to ensure the election of supporters.

He highlighted his attendance at the **Lausanne Conference**, even though he attended for only two days. His most significant foreign policy adventure, however, was the Corfu Incident. In August 1923 an Italian general, Tellini, was murdered on the Greek island of Corfu. Mussolini used the event to militarily occupy Corfu. He acted in defiance of the **League of Nations**, having already broken part of the peace treaties of 1919/20. Eventually, he was forced to withdraw, not by the League, but by the Conference of Ambassadors of European States. However, the Greeks paid the Italians 50 million lira in compensation. The Corfu Incident won Mussolini considerable praise at home as a man who defied the peace treaties that had created the 'mutilated victory' of 1919/20.

Mussolini also continued to use violence and intimidation to consolidate his political power. In December 1922 he turned the Fascist militia into Italy's national militia (MSVN), which acted as a political police force. During 1923 three opposition deputies were murdered and fifty physically attacked. Fascist violence reached its pinnacle during the elections of April 1924. To ensure his dominance over parliament Mussolini had passed the Acerbo Law in July 1923, which changed the electoral system so that any political party obtaining 25 per cent of the vote received 66 per cent of the seats in the Chamber. During the election campaign the MSVN attacked opposition meetings and supporters and destroyed their offices. Mussolini also **gerrymandered** electoral boundaries. As a result, the PNF received 374 seats against the opposition's 180 seats, mainly PSI and Communists. Throughout the campaign, Mussolini attempted to give the impression that he was unaware of the excesses of Fascist violence. However, there is evidence that he orchestrated much of what occurred. One incident almost cost him his position as Prime Minister: the murder of Socialist deputy, Giacomo Matteotti.

The Matteotti Affair (1924)

Giacomo Matteotti was the foremost opponent of Mussolini, who made outspoken attacks on Fascist violence. On 10 June 1924, he was murdered by a Fascist gang known as the Ceka (after the Soviet Terror Police), which was led by Dumini and Volpi. On the following day, Mussolini publically expressed his innocence in the affair. Italian historian Renzo de Felice claims that the murder took place without Mussolini's knowledge, although there is sufficient evidence to suggest that he knew. The Ceka had acted on the advice of two leading PNF members, Cesare Rossi and Filippo Marinelli, both close associates of Mussolini. Also, under Mussolini's orders, the Chamber of Deputies were prevented from meeting to discuss the affair. As a result, the PSI, PPI, Communists and many Liberal deputies withdrew from parliament in what was termed the

Aventine Secession: after the actions of politicians in Ancient Rome who went to the Aventine hill outside Rome to express their opposition to policy.

Aventine Secession.

Mussolini survived the Matteotti affair for a number of reasons. First, the Pope disassociated himself from the actions of the PPI. Secondly, opposition was controlled through a programme of intimidation by the MSVN, which led to the withdrawal of deputies who opposed Mussolini, thus making it easier for him to deal with parliament. Therefore, on 24 June, only 21 out of 398 senators voted against Mussolini over the affair. Thirdly, Mussolini could have been dismissed by the King, who refused to act. Finally, on 3 January 1925, in front of a parliament packed with his supporters, Mussolini announced that he took full responsibility for the Matteotti affair. Mussolini's survival ultimately depended on the support of the senate, the King, the Pope and the Italian people. He had achieved his ambition of becoming dictator and had ensured that once in power he had no intention of leaving it.

How did he become dictator of Italy?

1. Read the following extract and answer the question.

Mussolini becomes Prime Minister

'Lacking as he did any experience of government, Mussolini was remarkably undaunted by the task confronting him, and the fact testifies to his ability and self-confidence. All his new ministers, except one taken from Facta's government, were equally inexperienced. At his first cabinet meeting he laid down his general policy-pacification, national discipline and budget economics. Many fascists were expecting him to discard the constitution and establish armed rule, but whatever he said to the contrary, he knew that he was in power not as a result of revolution, but following a series of compromises with the King and representatives of the former liberal regime.'

(from Denis Mack Smith's *Mussolini*, Weidenfeld and Nicolson, 1981)

Using the extract above, and information from this section, how far was it true to say that in October 1922, Mussolini was given power rather than seizing it?

2. What do you regard as the most important reason why Mussolini was able to become dictator of Italy by 1925?

Was Mussolini's Italy a totalitarian dictatorship?

Was Fascist Italy the personal dictatorship of Mussolini?

How repressive was his dictatorship?

How successful were his social and economic policies?

Framework of events

1925	Mussolini declared his dictatorship
	Dopolavoro (OND) created
	Battle for Grain began
1926	Balilla Youth Movement created
	Ministry of Corporations established
	Special tribunal for political crimes created
	Created the secret police (OVRA)
1927	Labour Charter
	Quota 90 introduced
1928	New Electoral Law introduced
1929	Lateran Treaties with Vatican
1933	IRI created
1937	Ministry of Popular Culture created
1938	Anti-Semitic laws introduced
1943	Mussolini dismissed by the King
1943–5	Social Republic of Salo

THE inter-war period in Europe (1918–39) saw the emergence of several totalitarian dictatorships of which the most notable were Hitler's Germany and Stalin's USSR. In their study, *Totalitarian Dictatorship and Autocracy* (1956), US political scientists K. Friedrich and Z. Brezinski do not mention Italy. In *The Origins of Totalitarianism* (1958), Hannah Arendt declares that 'Mussolini's fascism, up to 1938, was not totalitarian but just an ordinary nationalist dictatorship, developed logically from multi-party democracy.' The Australian historian R. J. B. Bosworth claims that Mussolini was 'the least of dictators, a hollow tyrant.' Yet the first time that the term 'totalitarian' was used in the inter-war period was in reference to Mussolini's regime. It was first used by socialists in their comparison of Fascism to previous governments. Mussolini often talked of the Fascist revolution, of creating a completely new type of state and society. But just how far was Fascist Italy a totalitarian state?

Was Fascist Italy the personal dictatorship of Mussolini?

'Totalitarian', in the Italian sense, seemed to mean the absolute rule of one man: Mussolini. In *Europe 1870–1991* (2004), T. Morris and D. Murphy declare that 'the end product of the Fascist revolution was the personalised dictatorship of Mussolini'. On the surface, this certainly seemed to be true. By 1929, Mussolini was not only Prime Minister, but also minister of eight out of thirteen departments.

Important posts held by Mussolini

Prime Minister: 1922–43
Minister of Foreign Affairs: 1924–9; 1932–6
Minister of the Interior: 1924 and 1926–43
Minister for the Colonies: 1924
Minister of War:1924–9
Minister for the Navy: 1926–9
Minister for the Air Force: 1925–9; 1933–43
Minister for Public Works: 1929
Minister for Corporations: 1926–9; 1932–6
Commandant General of the Militia
Commandant General of the Armed Forces
First Marshal of the Empire
Chair of:
    Supreme Commission for Defence
    Council of State
    Court of Accounts
    Army Council
    Supreme Council of Statistics
    Permanent Committee on Cereal Production
    Committee on Civilian Mobilisation
    National Council of Corporations
    Fascist Grand Council

National Council of Corporations: contained corporations representing aspects of economic life. Each corporation contained representatives of business and labour. The aim was to find a 'third way' between dominance of business and dominance of labour. It was the equivalent of an economic parliament.

Mussolini was also *Il Duce* of the PNF, and he presided over the Fascist Grand Council and the **National Council of Corporations**.

In an interview, Mussolini declared that 'a leader can have no equals, no friends and give his confidence to no one.' He certainly gave the outward appearance of a dictator. In reality, however, although he was heavily built, he was below average height at 5' 6". He tried to disguise his shortness by standing very straight with his head lent back and his jaw jutting out. At official functions he preferred to stand next to the King, who was much shorter. He liked to wear military uniforms and had a love of fast cars, horse riding and flying. He tried to epitomise the idea of a virile, healthy ruler, but from 1925 his health deteriorated and, suffering from stomach ulcers, he was forced to follow a strict diet. Late in 1920, he went grey and subsequently shaved his head. Despite the fact that he insisted upon having at least nine hours sleep every night and refused to be disturbed for any reason, he was a hard and methodical administrator.

Mussolini shows off his physical prowess to a crowd.

Achille Starace (1889–1945)
He came from a middle class family in southern Italy and was a war hero in the First World War. In 1927, he was Vice Secretary of the PNF, and became Secretary from December 1931 until October 1939. He supported the idea of enrolling millions of ordinary Italians into the PNF. In particular, he was in favour of using sport and demonstrations to encourage support for Fascism. On 28 April 1945, he was captured by Italian communist partisans near Milan, executed, and his body hung upside down, next to Mussolini's, in Milan's main square.

The image of Mussolini as an all-knowing, dynamic leader was enhanced by his effective use of propaganda.

The cult of *Il Duce* became a central feature of the regime. Italians were extolled to *'Obedere, Credere, Combatere'* ('Believe! Obey! Fight!'). On 12 December 1931, the PNF Secretary, **Achille Starace**, introduced the ritual of *Saluto al Duce* ('Salute to the Leader') at the start of all PNF meetings. Mussolini's apparent invincibility was enhanced by his survival of three assassination attempts in 1926. Denis Mack Smith in *Mussolini, Artist in Propaganda* (1959) claims that because of this, Mussolini actually ended up believing his own publicity.

In *Italian Fascism* (1989), Alexander De Grand claims that Mussolini's dictatorship went through two distinct phases: one of consolidation (1925–35) and one of decline (1935–43). Renzo de Felice entitled the two volumes of Mussolini's biography, which cover 1936 to 1943, *The Totalitarian State* (1981), implying that there was a change in policy from that date. In its next phase, the regime is seen as having been more dependent on the 'myth' of Mussolini.

Landmark Study The book that changed people's views

Renzo de Felice: *Mussolini the Fascist* (Einaudi, 1965–1997)

Italian historian Renzo de Felice's monumental biography of Mussolini. The final volume was published posthumously. The biography includes: *The Revolutionary 1883–1920* (1965); *The Conquest of Power, 1921–1925* (1966); *The Organisation of the Fascist State, 1925–1929* (1968); *Years of Consensus, 1929–1936* (1974); *The Totalitarian State in two volumes, 1936–1940* (1981); *Italy at War, the Ally: 1940–1943;* and the *Civil War* *1943–1945* (1997). De Felice was Professor of History at the University of Salerno, and editor of the historical review *Storia Contemporanea* ('Contemporary History'). He developed what he regarded as anti anti-Fascist history. Before de Felice's studies of Mussolini and Fascist Italy, similar texts were written mainly from an anti-Fascist viewpoint. De Felice believed that Mussolini remained a genuine revolutionary until 1920, when he opted for right-wing politics. Using Italian archives, de Felice wrote over 2100 pages for the first three volumes of the biography, which covered the period up to 1929. He regarded Fascist Italy up to 1936 as authoritarian rather than totalitarian. To De Felice, Mussolini was an opportunist who made decisions 'suddenly, without adequate preparation'. He believed that from 1936 to 1943 Mussolini became a real totalitarian.

Totalitarian Dictatorship

In 1956, C. Friedrich and Z. Brezinski outlined what they saw as the key characteristics of a totalitarian dictatorship:

■ A charismatic leader with an elaborate ideology

■ A one-party state

■ A terror police force

■ Complete state control of education, culture and propaganda

■ Complete state control of the economy

■ Complete state control of the armed forces.

Cabinet: the senior committee of government.

Mussolini secured control through a 'divide and rule' tactic. In 1923, he established the Fascist Grand Council, which shared decision-making with the **cabinet**. Mussolini was the link between these two bodies. Also, Mussolini had no serious rivals. This is outlined by Denis Mack Smith, who claims that most of the leading Fascists were 'unintelligent, grasping, jealous and incompetent, and jockeyed for positions by telling tales against their rivals'. However, he is seen to have had limited control over the King, Catholic Church and to some extent the Fascist Party.

Relations with the King

Even though Mussolini was dictator, a constitutional monarchy still remained in existence and the King had the right to dismiss Mussolini at any time. On a number of critical occasions – most notably during the Matteotti affair of 1924 – he had the chance to do so, but declined. The King was never willing to confront the 'Fascist revolution in government' before the Second World War because the alternative may well have been chaos, and the rise to power of socialism. Although his relationship with the King was never very friendly, Mussolini always showed due respect. The King even remarked that Mussolini was one of his most respected Prime Ministers.

However, relations became strained in March 1938, when Mussolini announced that he had made himself First Marshal of the Italian Empire, a post without precedent and which had a quasi-royal dimension. The King made it clear to Mussolini that he disliked this development, but he acceded to Mussolini's decision to replace him as Commander-in-Chief of the Italian armed forces in times of war. Finally, however, it was the King who on 25 July 1943 dismissed Mussolini as Prime Minister.

Relations with the Vatican and Italian Catholic Church

One of Mussolini's greatest domestic achievements was the settlement between the Italian State and the Vatican, which Mussolini himself claimed was his most memorable triumph.

Papal States: the last part of the Papal States, the Patrimony of St Peter, with Rome as it capital, became part of the Italian state in 1870. From that moment on the Pope lost his political independence. Technically, he became an Italian citizen. It started a period known as the 'Babylonian captivity of the Papacy'.

The creation of an Italian State between 1859 and 1870 had resulted in a major crisis in Church–State relations. Up to 1870 the Pope had had two roles: spiritual head of all Catholics throughout the world, and ruler of an Italian State, the **Papal States**. Pope Pius IX (1846–78) refused to recognise the Italian State and instructed Catholics not to participate in Italian politics. However, an improvement in Church–State relations occurred in 1919 when Pope Benedict XV (1914–22) allowed the creation of the Catholic Political Party, (PPI).

Mussolini and Church Dignitaries posing at the Lateran Palace, Rome, after the signing of the Concordat (1929).

It took Mussolini – who as a young man was anti-clerical – to bring about a settlement. Negotiations between the government and the Vatican began in August 1926. Francesco Pacelli, whose brother became Pope Pius XII in 1939, represented the Vatican; Domenico Barone represented the government. By 11 February two agreements were reached.

The first agreement was the Lateran Treaty, between the Italian State and the Pope, which granted the Pope a small independent state within Rome, known as the Vatican City State. In return, the Pope recognised the Kingdom of Italy, and Victor Emmanuel III as King. This re-established the Pope's independence, which he had lost in 1870. The Pope also received 750 million lira in cash and one billion lira in government bonds as compensation for property taken from the Vatican. The second agreement between the Italian State and the Catholic Church was the **Concordat**, which determined the role of the Catholic Church within the Fascist state. The Concordat dealt mainly with education and marriage: the government extended Catholic religious instruction in schools from primary to secondary level; text books had to be approved by the Church; and religious marriages were recognised by the government. Mussolini also agreed to the independence of the youth section of Catholic Action.

Concordat: an agreement between an independent state and the Vatican about Church–State relations.

This agreement with the Church was important to Mussolini for a number of reasons. First, it increased the regime's popularity with Catholics. Secondly, it was an important factor in the overwhelming support given to Mussolini in the March 1929 referendum. Thirdly, it brought the Catholic Church within the Fascist regime in Italy. Finally, it increased Mussolini's international standing as a statesman, in Catholic countries in particular.

This does not mean that relations between Church and State were always cordial after 1929. In fact, a major rift occurred in 1931 when Mussolini attempted to disband the youth section of Catholic Action. On 9 July 1931, the government declared the merger of the youth section of Catholic Action with the Fascist youth movement, the *Ballila*. The Pope issued an **encyclical** *Non abbiamo bisogno* ('We have no need') against the declaration. Through an intermediary, Father Tacchi-Venturi, the Pope threatened to excommunicate Mussolini if he did not revoke this declaration. Thus on 2 September, the government announced that the youth section of Catholic Action would remain independent but would not compete in sporting activities, limiting itself instead to educational and religious matters.

Encyclical: a pronouncement by the Pope.

Another rift occurred in 1938 over the government's introduction of anti-Semitic laws. Mussolini's increasingly close relationship with Adolf Hitler was responsible for this complete change in

Fascist policy. On 3 August 1938, the Ministry of Education was prohibited from allowing foreign Jews (refugees) into schools. On 1 September Mussolini issued a decree forbidding foreign Jews to settle in Italy, Libya or the Dodeconese Islands and, the following day, all Jews were dismissed from teaching posts. Finally, on 6 October, the Fascist Grand Council announced that Italians would not be allowed to marry Jews and that Jews were forbidden to join the PNF or the armed forces. In Milan, **Cardinal** Shuster condemned these laws in a pastoral letter to all Catholics in his archdiocese. The Pope, who was a strong critic of Nazi Germany, also condemned Mussolini's policies against the Jews.

Cardinal: a senior cleric of the Catholic Church who has the right to elect the Pope.

Relations between the Vatican and Mussolini only improved from March 1939 when Pius XI died and was replaced by Pius XII (1939–58). Pius XII had been Papal Nuncio to Nazi Germany and had signed a concordat with Hitler.

Relations with the Fascist Party (PNF)

The Fascist movement, and from November 1921 the Fascist Party (PNF), had been a coalition of different interests. The moderate Fascists were willing to tolerate Mussolini's adoption of the constitutional path to power; extreme Fascists simply yearned for a Fascist revolution. From 1925 Mussolini brought the PNF under effective central control. Under the secretariat of Roberto Farinacci (1925/6) dissent within the PNF was silenced. Farinacci was an ex-railway worker and socialist with a violent and erratic personality. Mussolini replaced him in 1926 with Augusto Turati, who ensured that regional power bases within the PNF were liquidated. On 9 December 1928, the Law on the Powers of the Grand Council made the Fascist Grand Council State-controlled under Mussolini's leadership. Turati was succeeded by Giovanni Giurati from October to December 1931, who was later replaced by Achill Starace who remained Secretary of the PNF until October 1939. Starace made sure that the PNF did not provide an alternative power base for any rival to Mussolini. Starace widened PNF membership to include ordinary workers and peasants, which diluted the control of Fascist regional bosses. By the outbreak of the Second World War, the PNF attracted careerists and job seekers rather than revolutionaries.

How repressive was Mussolini's dictatorship?

Having announced a dictatorship in his speech to Parliament on 3 January 1925, Mussolini spent the next two years creating one. On

21 November 1925 he began by reintroducing capital punishment for treason. On 26 November, a law was issued governing all associations within Italy: all associations had to register with the police, as did their members; any breach of the law would lead to the closing of the association. This law applied to all political parties, and by November 1926, all deputies of the opposition had been expelled from parliament.

On 24 December 1925, a law decreed that any public servant could be dismissed for disloyalty to the government. On the same day, the post of Prime Minister was also changed to Head of Government. This meant that Mussolini reported to the King and not Parliament. On 31 January 1926, Mussolini acquired the power to rule by decree. In other words, he could make his own laws. A decree law passed on 31 December made newspaper owners liable for their editorial. It also created a journalists' association from which all anti-Fascists were excluded. All of these laws were reinforced by fascist violence. In *The Rise of the Fascist State* (1974), Italian historian Alberto Aquarone describes the 'intense campaign of intimidation, violence, confiscation, and suspension [that] was waged against the opposition press, which was finally reduced to silence. The squads also stepped up their attacks … [and the] police also intervened with ever-increasing frequency, issuing warning and ordering suspensions. The Italian press was completely muzzled.'

On 31 January 1926, a law was passed that denied Italian citizenship to anyone who committed an act that disturbed public order. Some of the first victims were Gaetano Salvemmi, an historian, and Giuseppe Donati, a Catholic journalist, who had both criticised the Fascists over the Matteotti affair. They subsequently lost all of their property. On 6 April 1926, a law extended central control over local government, and a subsequent law of 7 July 1926 abolished all local elections.

Thus by the end of 1926, Mussolini had removed the two main areas of opposition to his rule: parliament and a free press. From 3 April 1926, all cinemas were ordered to show official government newsreels, which were merely fascist propaganda. By 1930, approximately 66 per cent of all newspapers were controlled by the Fascists, and those newspapers that were not under their control received daily instructions on what to write on political matters.

In December 1926, the 'Law for the Defence of the State' was passed, which created a secret police and a special tribunal for political crimes. Arturo Bochinni was given the task of organising this secret political police force, OVRA. Bochinni served as chief of OVRA from 1926 to 1940 and was regarded as the third most powerful man in Italy after Mussolini and the King. Historians Denis Mack Smith and R. J. B. Bosworth claim that the name OVRA was chosen by Mussolini because it sounded sinister. However, in *Fascist Italy* (1968), Alan Cassels states that it stood for *Opera Volontaria per la Repressione Anti-fascista* ('Organisation for the Repression of Anti-Fascism'). In its operation, OVRA was far less oppressive than other security police, such as the Gestapo and SS in Nazi Germany, or OGPU and NKVD in Stalin's USSR; it was also rather small, employing just 375 staff. An important punishment used by OVRA was *confino* where the victim was forced to live either on the Lipari Islands, north of Sicily; on the isles of Tremiti off the Adriatic coast; or on the mainland at Amalfi and Cava dei Tirreni. However, although the penal settlement on the Lipari islands was hard, elsewhere internees were lodged in cottages of their own choice.

The special tribunal and OVRA were used simultaneously. In all 13 547 cases that were dealt with by 1943, 27 742 years of imprisonment were imposed. Between 1927 and 1943, the Fascist regime imposed 42 death sentences for political crimes, of which 31 were carried out, 22 of these during the Second World War. Ethnic groups that suffered particular persecution were Slovenes in the Trieste area, and after 1938, Jews.

It would seem on the surface that Mussolini's dictatorship, although repressive, was popular. On 24 March 1929, a referendum on the regime was held. More than 8.5 million people voted 'yes' in support of the regime; only 135 000 people voted 'no', with 8092 spoilt ballot papers.

The importance of propaganda and leisure

Mussolini once remarked that governing the Italian people wasn't hard: 'To govern them you need two things, policemen and bands playing in the streets.' Like other dictators, Mussolini used propaganda and sport to encourage support for the regime. State newsreels extolling the virtues of Fascism were seen in all cinemas. The press was effectively controlled. Government policies, such as the draining of the **Pontine Marshes** near Rome, received massive publicity. The archeological sites of ancient Rome were restored, causing much damage to Renaissance buildings.

Mussolini was also aware of the importance of sport. In 1934, the Italian football team won the World Cup when it was held in Rome. In Paris, in 1938, they repeated their performance. Also, the Italian Primo Carnera won the World Heavyweight Boxing title in 1933.

Pontine Marshes: the most famous area of the 'battle for land' reclamation scheme, which provided hundreds of thousands of acres of new farmland.

These sporting victories were exploited by the regime as examples of the superiority of Fascism.

An important factor in Mussolini's ability to maintain control was *Dopolavoro* ('for the sake of labour'), a fascist after-work organisation created in May 1925. It was the principal means by which Mussolini regulated the leisure hours of the adult, working population. It covered virtually everything that could be classed as 'mass culture': from sporting events to movies, from listening to the radio to going to the theatre. Membership, which rose from 300 000 in 1926 to 3.5 million in 1939, was voluntary. This comprised 40 per cent of the industrial workforce and 25 per cent of the peasantry. By the outbreak of war in 1940, the OND (Opera Nationzale Dopolavoro) ran 1227 theatres, 771 cinemas, 2130 orchestras, 6427 libraries and 11 500 sporting groups. It was the most popular Fascist organisation.

How successful were Mussolini's social and economic policies?

There is much debate as to whether Mussolini had clear aims in his economic policy. He certainly inherited a number of serious economic problems, most notably a sizeable budget deficit and an unemployment level of 500 000. Therefore, his aim when he came to power in 1922 was to create economic stability.

Initially, economic policy was placed under the control of Alberto Di Stefano, a liberal economist. His policies included abolishing price fixing and rent controls, and reducing government spending where possible. By 1925, he had successfully reduced unemployment to 122 000, and the government was in surplus. In July 1925, Di Stefano was replaced by Giuseppe Volpi, who settled Italy's war debts with the USA and Britain, and obtained a US loan of 100 million dollars.

Mussolini controlled the Italian economy through government intervention. However, historian Alexander De Grand argues in *Italian Fascism* (1989) that although the regime 'altered the role of the state in Italian economic life ... these changes were largely forced on the regime by events rather than implemented by any preconceived plan'. The first government economic policy was the introduction of **protectionism**. In August 1926, the government also imposed an exchange rate of 90 lira to the pound, which made the Italian currency seem more powerful. However, this made Italian exports more expensive and increased Italy's economic difficulties long before the **Wall Street Crash** caused a world economic depression at the end of 1929.

Protectionism: the placing of duties or quotas on imports to protect domestic industries against foreign competition.

Wall Street Crash (1929): the collapse of the share prices at the New York Stock Exchange in October 1929, which precipitated a worldwide economic depression.

Economic Indices for Italy: 1929–38		
1938 = 100		
Year	Industrial Production	Cost of living
1929	90	102
1930	85	99
1931	77	90
1932	77	87
1933	82	82
1934	80	78
1935	86	85
1936	86	85
1937	100	93
1938	100	100

The most innovative aspect of economic policy was the so-called creation of the Corporate State. Mussolini had always claimed that he was against class conflict between workers and employers; the Corporate State was meant to act as a model for economic and industrial harmony by uniting Italian Society. This began in 1926 when Guiseppe Bottai created a Ministry of Corporations, which controlled various branches of economic activity including industry, agriculture and commerce. In 1930, a National Council of Corporations drew together employer and worker organisations, which by 1934 had been refined and developed into mixed corporations of workers and employers. Finally, in 1939, a Chamber of Fasces and Corporations was established to which corporations sent representatives. It meant to settle industrial disputes equitably between employer and worker, but in reality it favoured the employer. This favouritism reinforced the dominance of business over labour. Free trade unions were abolished and replaced by fascist equivalents, which meant that all disputes were to be settled under the guidance of the Fascist State. The statutory eight-hour day was replaced by a nine-hour day. In the following year, the Charter of Labour was introduced, which referred all labour disputes to a labour court appointed by the Government. Finally, it made work 'a social duty'; voluntary withdrawal of labour (a strike) became a punishable offence.

Mussolini sows the first seeds in the new province of Littoria, which was reclaimed from the Pontine Marshes in the 'battle for land'.

An important Fascist economic institution was the *Instituto per la Reconstruzione Industriale* (Institution for the Reconstruction of Industry or IRI), set up in 1933. It was a state-financed body for helping weak companies to survive the economic depression. However, it favoured large businesses, taking many into public ownership. By 1939, 70 per cent of iron production, 45 per cent of steel production, 80 per cent of naval construction, and almost all shipping and parts of the electrical and telephone industries were taken over by the IRI.

Mussolini always couched economic initiatives in military language. In June 1925, he launched the 'battle for grain', aimed at reducing dependence on imports by increasing domestic production. This was quite an effective policy, reducing imports by 75 per cent by 1940. In 1927, the 'battle for the lira' created **Quota 90**. Finally, the 'battle for births' aimed to increase the Italian population by reducing emigration and increasing the birth rate. The population increased from 37.5 million in 1921 to 44.4 million in 1941.

Quota 90: the decision to change the international value of the lira from 150 to the pound to 90.46 to the pound sterling, which Mussolini believed showed Italy's economic stength. In reality, it made Italian exports more expensive and imports cheaper.

Autarky: economic self-sufficiency.

Mussolini's ultimate aim for economic policy was **autarky**. This was accelerated after 1936 when the League of Nations placed economic sanctions on Italy for invading Ethiopia. The economy grew at a yearly average of only 0.8 per cent between 1925 and 1940, compared to 3.8 per cent between 1900 and 1925, and 3.5 per cent

Real wages: the money a person receives when inflation (rising prices) has been removed. It refers to the 'purchasing powers' of wages.

between 1940 and 1952. This was partly due to the economic depression after 1929. The index of **real wages** fell 11 per cent between 1925 and 1938. In the countryside too, no significant changes occurred. In 1930, the peasantry comprised 87 per cent of the population but owned only 13 per cent of the land. Overall, the average per-capita income of Italians fell from 3079 lira in 1929 to 1829 lira by 1934. Unemployment also rose to one million by 1933.

Unfortunately, Italy's economic growth under Fascism was one of the slowest in the twentieth century. Compared to its competitors (Britain, Germany, France and the USSR), Italian economic development was limited. In 1940, the Italian economy was still in a weak state and unable to meet the demands of war effectively, an important factor in the Italian defeat.

Italian historian Cesare Vannutelli sums up Fascist economic policy in *The Living Standard of Italian Workers, 1929–1939* (1958) when he states:

'Italy suffered more than other countries from the world crisis of 1930–2 because its economy had already been weakened by the revaluation of the currency (Quota 90 in 1927). Unlike other countries, Italy could not benefit from economic recovery in the 1930s because of the policy of autarky. Consequently, Italy's economic development lagged behind that of other countries.'

The impact of Fascism on youth

The fascist regime placed great emphasis on the indoctrination of the Italian youth. Every attempt was made to incorporate youth into the party and state structure. On 3 April 1926, the *Opera Nazionale Ballila* ('National Youth Organisation') was created for young people aged six to 18 years. The aim was to organise activities outside of school hours. In 1930, the *Fascio Giovanile del Littori* ('Fascist Juvenile Group') was set up for 18 to 21 year-olds. At university level, a separate organisation, the *Gruppo Universitari Fascisti*, aimed to sustain fascist propaganda. However, its membership was small and unenthusiastic. Nevertheless, these organisations were central to Fascism's attempt to reach the mass of the Italian population. In October 1937, all youth movements were unified as the *Gioventu Italiano del Littorio* ('Italian Fascist Youth' or GIL) under the control of the PNF. By 1939 the two youth movements had eight million members.

Impact on education

The regime also altered the education system to ensure its influence. In every classroom a portrait of the King had to be accompanied by one of Mussolini. University professors were forced to take an oath of loyalty to the regime. School textbooks were altered to emphasise the 'cult of *Il Duce*'. In a compulsory textbook for eight year-olds it stated that 'the eyes of Il Duce are on every one of you. A child who asks Why? is like a bayonet made of milk. You must obey because you must. What is the duty of a child? Obedience!'

Impact on women

Radical social change was not only limited to youth. Fascism also had a major impact on women. In their Programme of 1919, the Fascists promised women the vote and social equality. However, this did not occur when they took power. With the 'battle for births' the regime constantly emphasised the role of women as home-makers, whose main function in life was to bring up children. 'Mother and Child Day' was introduced and became officially recognised from 1933. To train future mothers, the *Piccole Italiane* (for girls aged nine to 14) and the *Giovani Italiane* (for girls aged 15 to 17) were set up. From the mid-1920s, a popular slogan of the PNF was *le donne e casa* ('women into the home'). This coincided with the creation of the *Opera Nazionale de Maternita e Infanzia* ('national organisation for child rearing' or OMNI), which supervised the welfare of mothers and children. From 1929, working mothers received maternity leave and welfare payments. Taxes were even placed on bachelors to encourage marriage. These developments received powerful support from the Catholic Church.

Giovanni Gentile, the Minister of Education from October 1922, restricted the numbers of female teachers in secondary schools. Preference was also given to men in government employment. In 1938 a law was passed limiting the number of women in the workforce to just 10 per cent. Women had their own organisation within the Fascist Party, the *Fasci di Femminili*, or women's auxiliaries. It published its own periodicals, *Giornale dell Donna* ('Mothers' Journal') from 1924, and *Vita Femminile* ('Female Life') from 1926. The aim of the organisation was to support fascist programmes on the family. By 1935, it had only 400 000 members compared to two million men in the PNF.

Republic of Salo

Following his rescue by German paratroops in September 1943, Mussolini created the Social Republic of Salo in German-occupied north Italy. From September 1943 until his death in April 1945, Mussolini presided over this German puppet-state. Real power resided in the hands of General Wolff of the German army. Mussolini declared that the Republic was against the traitors who had ousted him in July 1925, including Fascists such as Grandi, the monarchy, the armed forces and the civil service. In reality, there was little difference between the policies that he followed before and after September 1943. His main support came from pro-Germans, anti-semites and the remnants of the PNF.

The Salo Republic had no capital. Foreign affairs were dealt with from Salo, defence from Cremona, Corporations from Verona, education from Padua, and justice from Brescia. It had neither an army nor any diplomatic recognition beyond Nazi Germany and its allies. The nearest it got to a constitution was the programme produced by the Verona Congress of the reformed PNF in November 1943. It was republican, pro-Catholic and anti-Semitic. In economic matters it promised a 'third way' between capitalism and socialism. Under a law of February 1944, all large businesses were placed under state control. In *Mussolini* (1981) Denis Mack Smith argues that in the Salo Republic, Mussolini 'reasserted the socialist beliefs of his youth', claiming that he had never deserted the Fascist programme of 1919, which contained a strong socialist core.

By late 1944 even Mussolini began to backtrack on his anti-Semitic policies, claiming that they were opportunist and had been a mistake. By early 1945 he was blaming the Germans for his predicament. He regarded Hitler as a fanatic and a 'thorough-going authoritarian'. He regarded himself as authoritarian 'only on the surface'. On 28 April, he suffered the ultimate humiliation of being captured and executed by Italian communist partisans and subsequently being displayed hanging upside-down in the main square of Milan where Fascism had been born in March 1919.

Was Mussolini's Italy a totalitarian dictatorship?

1. Read the following extract and then answer the question.

   ### Fascist rule

   'Since 1922 Italy has been living under a dictatorship. For 12 years Italy has enjoyed a government established by force and maintained by force and by the exclusion of all alternative opinions. The word democracy must be left out of the question altogether. The Italian regime is a dictatorship. Fascism is Mussolini: that is the judgement of most Italians. It has all his strength and weakness and while he is great he is mortal. Fascism will perish with Mussolini, leaving as a heritage the problem of establishing a government suitable for the average Italian. This can hardly be accomplished peacefully.'

   (Adapted from Herman Finer's *Mussolini's Italy*,
   Victor Gollanz Press, 1935, page 11.)

   Using the extract above, and information from this section, how far do you agree that Fascist rule was the personal rule of Mussolini?

2. To what extent did Fascism control the lives of all Italians from 1925 to 1945?

3 | Foreign policy: creating a new Roman Empire?

What were his foreign policy aims?

Was the Ethiopian War the major turning point in foreign policy?

Was he Hitler's puppet?

Timeline of Events

1923	Corfu Incident
1924	Italy annexed Fiume
1925	Italy signed the Locarno Treaties
1926	Italy occupied Albania
1934	Nazis fail in their attempt to unite Germany and Austria
1935	Stresa Front against German conscription and rearmament
	Italy invaded Ethiopia
1936	Outbreak of Spanish Civil War. Italy sent aid to Franco
	Rome-Berlin Axis
1937	Anti-Comintern Pact with Germany and Japan
1938	*Anschluss* of Germany and Austria
	Munich Crisis
1939	Italy annexed Albania
	Pact of Steel
	Germany invaded Poland, Second World War begins
1940	Italy declared war on Britain and France
1941/2	Italy defeated in Ethiopia and Libya
1943	Sicily and mainland Italy invaded by Allies
	Mussolini sacked by King
1943–5	Social Republic of Salo in north Italy

MUSSOLINI'S foreign policy is a matter of considerable debate among historians. When he came to power as Prime Minister in October 1922, some of his biographers, such as Denis Mack Smith, claim that he did not have a clear aim in his foreign affairs. Rather, Mussolini is portrayed as an opportunist. However, important questions require discussion. Were Mussolini's foreign policy aims merely a continuation of the policies pursued by his liberal predecessors? Or, was there a distinct Fascist foreign policy? German historian, Fritz Fischer, highlighted how domestic issues influenced the agenda for foreign affairs. How far were Mussolini's foreign ventures dictated by domestic concerns? Was he the peacemaker of Europe, or an aggressor who destabilised inter-war Europe, making the Second World War more likely? Was Mussolini's foreign policy racist? Finally, was there a turning point in Mussolini's foreign policy at which it became more aggressive and expansionist? These questions are central not only to any study of Mussolini, but also for studies of Italian and European history. The Second World War plunged the European continent into six years of carnage. During the war, Italy lost its entire overseas empire, was invaded, and suffered a two-year civil war. Mussolini clearly played a pivotal role in these events.

What were Mussolini's foreign policy aims?

In *Italian Fascism* (1989), historian Alexander De Grand claims that 'when the fascist government took power in October 1922, little thought had been given to foreign policy'. Yet one of the reasons why Mussolini split from the PSI in 1914 was because of foreign affairs. Mussolini's decision to support Italy's entry into the First World War on the side of the Allies was the major turning point in his political career.

Canadian historian, Alan Cassels, supports the view that foreign affairs were, in fact, central to Mussolini's thinking. In *Fascist Italy* (1969), he claims that 'the drive for a totalitarian society was nothing more or less than an endeavour to escape dependence on foreign powers. In the last resort Italy's international status was the criterion by which Mussolini's regime would stand or fall.' Mussolini's main aim was to obtain international advantage for Italy, which would reflect on his position as *Il Duce*. Australian historian, R. J. B. Bosworth expands on this in *Mussolini* (2002) when he claims:

'from the beginning of his career Mussolini had mostly directed his aspiration to be a 'Great Man' by advertising his expertise in international affairs. This is reflected by Mussolini's personal

Denis Mack Smith, *Mussolini's Roman Empire* (Arnold, 1976)

Denis Mack Smith has been the foremost British historian on Mussolini. His biography of Mussolini, written in 1981, stands out as one of the most significant studies of *Il Duce* in the English speaking world. However, in 1976 his *Mussolini's Roman Empire* was a significant milestone in the study of Italian foreign and imperial policy during the Fascist era. Mack Smith emphasises the pragmatic and opportunistic nature of Mussolini's policies. He claims that just as Mussolini lacked any real attachment to principle when he rose to power, he also lacked principles when he engaged in foreign and imperial affairs. However, Mack Smith believes that Mussolini's early life, where he witnessed and engaged in brutality and violence, explain Mussolini's innate aggressiveness in foreign affairs, in particular after 1931.

Count Galaezzo Ciano (1903–44)
He took part in the March on Rome in October 1922, and rose to a high position within the Fascist Party (PNF). In 1930, he married Mussolini's eldest daughter, Edda. He acted as Minister for the Press and Propaganda (1934) and Foreign Minister (1936). He tried to negotiate peace with the Allies from 1942, and was a member of the Fascist Grand Council that deposed Mussolini in July 1943. He was executed for treason against Mussolini.

involvement. For most of his regime he had direct control over the ministry of Foreign Affairs. In the 1930s he worked closely with his son-in-law, **Count Galaezzo Ciano**. Mussolini also had control over the ministries associated with the armed forces. In the 1930s he also took on another political title, 'First Marshal of the Empire.'

In *Hitler's Italian Allies* (2000), McGregor Knox believes that 'like Hitler, Mussolini believed he was a man of destiny whose task in life was to make Italy 'respected and feared' in international affairs.'

The merger between the Fascists (PNF) and Nationalists in 1923 led to important developments in Mussolini's foreign policy, which involved the acquisition of many of the Nationalist Party's aims. Part of the merger agreement involved Mussolini adopting a more aggressive foreign policy, supported by strong armed forces.

Indeed, Denis Mack Smith's study of Mussolini's foreign policy suggests that he wanted to recreate a modern Roman Empire by expanding Italy's colonial territories in East Africa. In 1922, Italy controlled Libya in North Africa and owned Italian Somaliland and Eritrea in East Africa. Ethiopia, which lay next to these Italian colonies, was an obvious target for Mussolini, particularly since there had been a long-standing feud concerning the exact border between Ethiopia and these territories. Mussolini believed that Ethiopia was within Italy's sphere of influence and hoped to reverse the humiliation that the nation had faced during the military defeat by the Ethiopians at the battle of Adowa in 1896. On a broader scale Mussolini hoped to acquire Anglo-Egyptian Sudan, thus uniting all his African territories into one geographical unit.

Italy's colonial ambitions were not limited to Africa. Mussolini also had aims to extend Italian power and influence around the Adriatic and the Balkans. His aim of making the Adriatic Sea an 'Italian lake' led him to apply diplomatic pressure on Yugoslavia to give him Fiume, which Italy felt they deserved as payment for their '**mutilated victory**'. It also involved acquiring Albania and undermining the Kingdom of Yugoslavia, which controlled the Dalmatian coast, by supporting Croat separatists who wished to break from Yugoslavia. This led, indirectly, to the assassination of King Peter of Yugoslavia and the French President by a Croat terrorist in Marseilles in 1934.

'**Mutilated victory**': the idea that Italy won the First World War but lost the peace. Italy did not receive all the territory promised to her by the Treaty of London in April 1915, which brought Italy into the war.

Mussolini also strove for Italian domination of the Mediterranean, which brought Italy into conflict with Britain. One of Mussolini's greatest achievements was the expansion and modernisation of the Italian Navy. This enabled Italy to acquire Malta (a British colony and

The extent of the Italian Fascist Empire in 1940.

naval base) and destabilise British influence in Egypt. The invasions of Greece and Egypt in late 1940 were also part of this strategy. Rather naively, Mussolini tried to persuade Hitler to abandon his ambitions towards the USSR and support Italy in its attempt to control the Mediterranean.

Aside from Mussolini's aim of expanding the Italian empire, domestic considerations were also important in his conduct of foreign policy. Improving Italy's international standing was seen as effective propaganda for increasing support for the regime. In *Mussolini's Roman Empire* (1976), Denis Mack Smith claims that Mussolini was glad to sign treaties because treaties meant news. From 1935 to 1936 the regime's popularity significantly increased because of the successful invasion of Ethiopia. Another domestic issue was the onset of the world economic depression in 1929. Italy, more than most other European states, was adversely affected. The development of a more aggressive foreign policy in the 1930s can be explained in part as diverting domestic attention away from economic concerns.

Mussolini's foreign policy aims: change or continuity?

Historians have long debated the degree to which foreign policy actually changed under Mussolini's control. Did he develop a unique Fascist foreign policy? Or, did Mussolini simply follow the same policy that had been set up by his liberal predecessors? In terms of his policy of colonial expansion, in *Mussolini* (2002) R.J.B. Bosworth is emphatic that:

> 'Even at its most aggressive, Fascist Italy behaved as though it were a nineteenth-century power, replicating the grab for Africa indulged by the Greater Powers at that time.'

He suggests that rather than break from his liberal past, Mussolini's aim to expand Italian influence simply continued the themes that had shaped Italian foreign policy before his rise to power. However, other historians have identified distinct Fascist characteristics in Mussolini's views on foreign affairs. In *Mussolini's Early Diplomacy* (1970), Alan Cassels claims that the Corfu Incident of August 1923 constituted a change from earlier policy. He believes that this incident – caused by the murder of an Italian general by Albanian terrorists on the Greek island of Corfu, which led the Italian navy to bombard Corfu – 'disclosed the nature of Fascism's foreign policy. It constituted a dress rehearsal for Mussolini's quarrel with the League of Nations over Ethiopia in 1935'.

A truly Fascist foreign policy can be seen to have developed in 1926 with the resignation of non-Fascist Salvatore Contarini, the Secretary General of the Foreign Ministry, after Dino Grandi, a leading Fascist, became involved with foreign affairs. The complete 'fascistization' of foreign affairs came from 1936, when Count Galaezzo Ciano, Mussolini's son-in-law, was appointed as Foreign Minister. From this time, foreign policy involved providing a tremendous amount of support for international Fascist-style movements. In *Mussolini's Roman Empire* (1976), Denis Mack Smith outlines how Mussolini allowed right-wing **paramilitary** groups, such as the Nazis, to train in Italy; gave support to the Heimwehr, a right-wing paramilitary movement in Austria; provided approximately 60 000 pounds per year to Oswald Mosley and the British Union of Fascists; and offered money to the 'Blueshirts', an Irish Fascist group. Mussolini also planned to destabilise the Kingdom of Yugoslavia by forming an alliance with Hungary and providing financial support for separatist movements in Macedonia and Croatia.

Paramilitary: an organisation that wears uniforms and engages in violence but is not an official armed military force.

The biggest display of this style of foreign policy was Mussolini's support for Franco and the Nationalists in the Spanish Civil War (1936–9), which Germany also supported. Mussolini supplied aircraft to transport Franco's troops from Spanish Morocco to mainland Spain in 1936. He also dispatched a large number of men and war material to support Franco over the duration of the war. By 1937, Italy had 35 000 men fighting in Spain in the *corpo truppo voluntaria* ('volunteer corps' or CTV). The degree of Italian intervention in the Spanish Civil War far exceeded that of Nazi Germany and the USSR (who supported the Republican side). By the end of the war, 3819 Italians had been killed and approximately 12 000 wounded. In monetary terms it had cost between 12 and 14 billion lira, equivalent to two years' military expenditure. This included the provision of 250 000 rifles, 2000 artillery guns and 750 aircraft for Franco's Nationalist cause, equal to a third of Italy's military might.

Was the Ethiopian War the major turning point in foreign policy?

Historians usually divide Mussolini's foreign policy into two distinct phases. In the 1920s Mussolini is portrayed as having followed a relatively passive foreign policy. While he still wanted to gain respect from the Great Powers, he was much more cautious in his approach. This is evident in his support of the Franco-Belgian occupation of the Ruhr, an industrial area of Germany, which occurred because Germany was late in paying reparations. Similarly, in 1925, Italy was also one of the major signatories of the Locarno Treaties, which confirmed Germany's post-1919 borders. The treaties were regarded as a major breakthrough in ensuring peace and stability in Europe. In 1928, Mussolini, along with most European countries, signed the Kellogg-Briand Pact, which renounced war as a diplomatic weapon. To a certain extent these policies were successful in increasing Mussolini's respectability, particularly from Britain. The British Foreign Secretary, Austen Chamberlain, believed that it was only a matter of time before Mussolini would become a moderate. This view was echoed by the British ambassador of Rome, Robert Graham. However, Denis Mack Smith believes that Mussolini, rather than being passive and cautious, used foreign policy as a propaganda exercise to further the cause of Italian Fascism abroad. This is especially apparent in Mussolini's suggestion of moving the secretariat of the League of Nations from Geneva to Rome.

During this period of passive foreign policy, Mussolini was also successful in his acquisition of the Adriatic port of Fiume, which many Nationalists had been demanding since the First World War. At the Paris Peace Conference, the Dalmatian coast, which the Allies had promised to Italy, was instead awarded to the newly created Kingdom of Yugoslavia. Italy only received the port in 1924, after it was seized and occupied by Gabriele D'Annunzio from 1919 to 1920, and following a period of diplomatic pressure by Italy.

Italian influence in the Adriatic also increased from November 1926 when King Zog of Albania signed a treaty, which gave Italy economic control of Albania. From 1927, Italian army officers trained the Albanian army. Italy later became responsible for Albania's administration. Eventually, in 1939 Albania was formally **annexed**, and King Zog deposed. Mussolini had also succeeded in controlling the Straits of Otranto, which formed the entrance to the Adriatic Sea from the Mediterranean.

Annex: to take over territory from another country.

Ceded: to give territory to another country.

In colonial affairs Mussolini achieved some success when in 1925 Britain **ceded** Jubaland to Italian Somaliland. Later, in March 1935, Italy also joined Britain and France to create the Stresa Front: an international attempt to defend the Treaty of Versailles against Germany's announcement to reintroduce military conscription.

During the 1930s Mussolini's foreign policy is considered to have become much more aggressive. The most obvious example of this was the invasion of Ethiopia. The reasons as to why this change occurred have caused much debate among historians. Biographer Renzo de Felice argues that the change occurred when Mussolini appointed leading Fascist, Dino Grandi, as Head of Foreign Affairs in 1929. Historian G. Carocci believes that changes in policy did not occur until later, over the period 1932 to 1935. In *Mussolini as Empire Builder* (1977), Esmonde Roberston offers a different explanation, placing emphasis on the death in December 1931 of Mussolini's younger brother, Arnaldo, who Roberston regards as having been a major restraining influence on Mussolini's naturally aggressive temperament. However, Roberston also cites an important meeting between Mussolini and Pope Pius XI on 11 February 1932 at which the Pope warned Mussolini about the growth in the influence of Protestants, Jews and Communists. Mussolini had just experienced a serious rift with the Vatican over the youth section of Catholic Action and the *Balilla*. In this way Mussolini's decision to extend Italy, and with it Catholic influence, can be seen as a way to appease the Pope. Several historians, including Roberston and Mack Smith, identify the economic depression in Italy as an important motivating factor in Mussolini's change in approach to foreign affairs. Success abroad would certainly have diverted attention away from growing economic problems.

Finally, as R. J. B. Bosworth points out, Mussolini can be seen to have fulfilled the traditional Italian policy of imperialism by reversing the defeat of Adowa of 1896 and conquering part of East Africa, which was within Italy's sphere of influence. Italy invaded Ethiopia on 3 October 1935 following a border incident at Wal Wal the previous year between Ethiopia and Italian Somaliland. Mussolini employed brutal methods including poison gas and the massacre of approximately 400 000 Ethiopians, and easily defeated the outdated Ethiopian Army.

The Ethiopian War can be seen as a turning point in Mussolini's overseas policy. Although the conquest gained him increasing prestige and popularity in Italy, it was condemned by the League of Nations who imposed economic sanctions on Italy. However, these sanctions were rather weak because they excluded key goods such as petroleum products. Furthermore, Britain did not close the Suez Canal to Italian shipping, which would have cut Italy off from Ethiopia, and the USA (which was not a member of the League of Nations) continued to trade with Italy. Despite this, however, Italy still made the decision to leave the League of Nations in 1937. In international terms this meant that Italy, along with Japan and Germany, was seen as a state that wished to upset international peace and stability.

The outbreak of war did not end attempts by British and French diplomats to woo Mussolini. In the secret **Hoare-Laval Plan** of 1935,

Hoare-Laval Plan (7–8 December 1935): named after British Foreign Secretary, Sir Samuel Hoare and French Foreign Minister, Pierre Laval. It planned to partition Ethiopia, leaving Ethiopian emperor Haile Selassi with some territory. The plan was rejected by the British and French governments on 18 December 1935, but not by Mussolini.

two senior British and French politicians attempted to appease Mussolini by offering Italy a partition of Ethiopia. However, once this 'pact' became public knowledge in Britain and France it caused outrage, and was subsequently dropped by both governments. Ultimately, the Ethiopian conquest signified the growing gulf between Italy and the western democracies and further aligned Italy with Germany.

A new direction in foreign affairs was signalled by the appointment of Mussolini's son-in-law Count Galeazzo Ciano as Minister of Foreign Affairs. Ciano paved the way for a closer relationship between Mussolini and Hitler, which was to have tragic consequences for Mussolini and Fascist Italy.

Some historians still regard Mussolini as Europe's peacemaker, even after 1935. In *Roma tra Londra e Berlino* (*Rome between London and Berlin*) (1980), Italian historian Rosaria Quartararo claims that Italy remained pivotal in ensuring European peace. She states that Mussolini was central in the achievement of the Munich agreement over Czechoslovakia in September 1938 and that the 'European war did not break out on 1 October 1938 only because Fascist Italy did not want to go to war.' Again in August/September 1939, as Hitler prepared to invade Poland, Mussolini is portrayed as trying to mediate between Germany, Britain and France. He is seen as the 'real arbiter' of the crisis. It was only on 9 June 1940, once Mussolini was convinced that Germany had defeated France and would shortly do the same to Britain, that he reluctantly committed Italy to war on Hitler's side.

Was Mussolini Hitler's puppet?

Mussolini's association with Hitler created the impression that the two right-wing dictators were united in a common ideological foreign policy. What historian F. W. Deakin called 'the Brutal Friendship' was born from Mussolini's decision to invade Ethiopia in October 1935. Up to that point, Mussolini had cooperated with powers such as Britain and France. In fact, Mussolini was exceedingly wary of Hitler's designs on Austria from 1933 to 1935 because he regarded Austria as within his own sphere of influence. In 1934, Austrian Nazis had attempted to seize power by assassinating the Austrian Prime Minister, Engelbert Dolfuss, an ally of Italy. To prevent a Nazi takeover, Mussolini moved four divisions of the Italian army to the Austro-Italian border and engaged in a propaganda campaign against them. Italian action was an important factor in preventing a German-Austrian union.

Comintern: the Communist International organisation set up in Soviet Russia in 1919 to spread the ideology of communism around the world.

Anschluss: the forcible union of Germany with Austria.

However, from October 1935 Mussolini became increasingly associated with Nazi Germany. In 1936, the Rome-Berlin Axis announced their mutual support. This collaboration was expanded to include Japan with the signing of the Anti-**Comintern** Pact in 1937. In December 1937, an economic agreement was concluded between Germany and Italy whereby Italy agreed to import more German manufactured goods. In return, Italy sent 30 000 agricultural labourers to work in Germany. By 1939 Italy had become increasingly dependent on Germany, for coal imports in particular.

By March 1938, when Hitler took control of Austria in the ***Anschluss***, Mussolini stood back and did nothing. On 22 May 1939 Germany and Italy consolidated their relationship with the Pact of Steel which brought the two Fascist powers into alliance. Italy agreed to commit all of its armed forces if Germany became involved in a war. Also, both sides agreed to consult each other if international events threatened war. However, Mussolini regarded the pact as 'yet another piece of paper' that had little bearing on future Italian action. Thus when the Second World War began on 3 September 1939, Mussolini decided to remain neutral. Finally,

Mussolini and Hitler watch a Nazi parade in 1937.

in June 1940 Mussolini joined Germany in its war against Britain and France. From that moment on Mussolini was tied to Hitler's shirt-tails. When Hitler launched **Operation Barbarossa** against the USSR in June 1941, Mussolini provided an Italian army to assist Germany and its other allies (Romania, Hungary and Finland). In Yugoslavia, Greece and North Africa, Italian and German troops fought side by side. When the war turned decisively in the Allies' favour after the battles of El Alamein (November 1942) in North Africa and Stalingrad (Sept. 1942 to Feb. 1943) on the Eastern Front, Mussolini's fate seemed sealed. The Anglo-American invasion and occupation of Sicily in July 1943 brought about Mussolini's downfall on 25 July that year.

Operation Barbarossa: the surprise attack on the USSR by Germany and its Allies from 22 June 1941.

Was Mussolini's foreign policy racist?

A controversial aspect of Mussolini's foreign policy that suggests a break with the past is the racism that occurred both in Italy's colonial territories and in its policies in Europe during the Second World War.

A central aim of Mussolini's foreign policy was to link Fascist Italy with the glory of the Roman Empire. Fascist propaganda always tried to make this link: the cult of *Il Duce* mirrored the adulation once heaped on Roman Emperors; the adoption of the Roman salute as the Fascist salute was an outward symbol of this association; the adoption of the Roman 'fasces' as the Fascist symbol – the axe surrounded by a bundle of sticks was the ancient Roman symbol of justice – was representative of Mussolini's vision of Italy as ruling inferior races, both in Africa and in the Balkans.

In many ways this mirrored the colonial ambitions of Italian governments prior to the First World War. However, there was a new intensity and brutality to Mussolini's policies. In Libya, between 1928 and 1933, the Italians used excessive force to subdue the resident Arab population. Under the Governorship of **General Badoglio**, the Italian colonial government engaged in a

General Pietro Badoglio (1871–1956)
Mussolini's Senior General, a Marshal of Italy and briefly Mussolini's successor in 1943. He was Army Chief of Staff from April 1925 and became Governor of Libya from September 1928 to December 1933, using extreme methods to quell a local Arab uprising. Although he initially opposed the Ethiopian War, he became Italian commander in Ethiopia from November 1936, and again in 1939/40. He led the failed invasion of Greece in 1940. He resigned on December 4 1940, following accusations of incompetence from leading Fascist, Roberto Farinacci. Following Mussolini's arrest on 25 July 1943, the King appointed him as Chief of Government. He negotiated a ceasefire with the Allies behind the backs of the Germans.

Ethnic cleansing:
describes the murder of a
population on the basis of
race. An alternative term is
genocide.

policy that would be now termed **ethnic cleansing**. In 1930, in a bid to end local opposition to Italian rule, the Italians drove out an Arab population of 100 000 from the interior. Displaced families were put in concentration camps on the Libyan coast. When the camps were closed in September 1933, only 50 per cent of the original inmates had survived. In fighting the local insurgent Omar al-Mukhtar, the Italians used poison gas. In September 1931, al-Mukhtar was put on trial and publicly hanged. In Ethiopia the Italians adopted similar tactics: poison gas, aerial bombardment of civilian targets, and indiscriminate massacres characterised the military campaign. **General Graziani** claimed: 'The Duce shall have Ethiopia with the Ethiopians or without them, just as he pleases'. Indro Montanelli, a Fascist journalist who fought in Ethiopia, proclaimed: 'We shall never be the dominators if we don't have an exact consciousness of our destined superiority. We do not mix with blacks. We cannot, we must not.' In July 1936, Mussolini appointed General Graziani as Viceroy of Ethiopia and gave him instructions to follow a policy of terror and extermination. Following a grenade attack by Ethiopian insurgents on 19 February 1937, the Italians retaliated by massacring over 3000 Ethiopians.

In Europe, Italian racism was also apparent. In Yugoslavia, Italian troops forced Orthodox Christian Serbs to convert to Catholicism. The Italians also supported the Ustace, the Croat military force that engaged in ethnic cleansing against the Serbs.

An even more problematic area of Mussolini's overseas policy was his association with the Holocaust. In 1938, the Fascist government introduced anti-Semitic laws. Italian Jews, unlike those of Eastern Europe, were integrated into mainstream society. By 1942 reports had reached Mussolini's government of the onset of **'The Final Solution'** against Jews in Poland. Although there is evidence that Italian officials were slow and obstructive in meeting German demands to hand over Jews in Tunisia, France

'The Final Solution': the German plan to murder the entire European population of Jews and Gypsies.

General Rodolpho Graziani (1882–1955)
Major colonial general, Chief of Staff and Minister of Defence in the Social Republic of Salo, 1943–5. He pacified Libya from 1932 to 1933 and was appointed Governor of Somaliland in 1935. He led the southern front in the Ethiopian War and was an extremely brutal colonial administrator. He was in charge of the Italian North African Army in December 1940 when it was routed by the British under General Wavell. He retired from the army in 1941 and received a 19-year prison sentence after the war, but only served his sentence until 1950 when he became head of the Neo-Fascist Party, the MSI.

and Yugoslavia, Mussolini eventually acceded to German demands on the issue. In June 1942, Italian troops engaged in a roundup of Jews in Croatia.

Following his dismissal by the King on 25 July, and the subsequent creation of the Republic of Salo, Mussolini's link with the Holocaust became clear. As a puppet of the German administration in north Italy, Mussolini had to accept the deportation of the Jews to the death camps in occupied Poland. By the spring of 1945, with his regime on the brink of collapse, Mussolini claimed that his racial policies had always been opportunistic and that he regretted his involvement in Hitler's anti-semitic campaign.

Was Mussolini a complete failure in foreign affairs?

Ultimately, Mussolini was overthrown because of his failures in foreign policy. Yet, during his regime, Italy's standing among the European powers increased. In many ways Mussolini did achieve his aim of making Italy a nation to be respected and feared – foreign affairs did aid the survival of his regime at home; the invasion and occupation of Ethiopia won support in 1936 from the Catholic Church, industrialists and nationalists. Italian philosopher, Giovanni Gentile claimed: 'Mussolini today has not just founded an empire in Ethiopia. He has made something more. He has created a new Italy.' Historian Renzo de Felice describes the conquest of Ethiopia as 'Mussolini's masterpiece'.

However, the Ethiopian War did not come without a cost: nearly an entire year's annual revenue for the government. In addition, the cost of replacing lost military equipment amounted to the equivalent of the military budget for three years. When combined with the cost of the Italian involvement in the Spanish Civil War, Mussolini's foreign adventures had almost bled Italy dry by 1939. Italy was the first major European state to rearm after the First World War. As a result, much Italian military equipment was obsolete by the outbreak of the Second World War. The lack of finance to engage in a modernisation programme after the Ethiopian War helps to explain Italy's poor military performance from 1940 to 1943.

The conquest of Ethiopia did not produce the economic benefits that Mussolini had hoped for. By 1941, only 3200 Italians had emigrated to Ethiopia. In its short life (1936–41) the Ethiopian Empire never ran at a profit. In the end, Mussolini's dream of a great East African Empire was short lived. In 1941, British troops from Kenya and Sudan overran the territory with relative ease. The War also forced Mussolini into a relationship with Hitler and so, from 1936 to 1943, Mussolini's fate in foreign and imperial affairs were dependent on Hitler's success. When Hitler failed to achieve his military aims in the Second World War, Mussolini was doomed.

Foreign policy: creating a new Roman Empire?

1. Read the following extract and answer the question.

   Mussolini's Foreign Policy Aims

   There is no doubt that Mussolini was moved by the desire to wipe out the memory of the defeat of the Italians by the Ethiopians at the Battle of Adowa, in 1896. But mingled with this desire for vengeance was the ambition to extend Italy's overseas possessions. The mirage of a modern Roman Empire beckoned.

   If he was to match the position of Britain and France in the world, he must also possess overseas territories, from which, so he argued, he could export his surplus population.

   Adapted from *Mussolini: Study of Demagogue*
   by Sir Ivone Kirkpatrick, Odhams Press, 1964, p292–3

   Using information from the above extract, and information from this section, what were Mussolini's aims in overseas policy?

2. How far did 1935 mark a turning point in Mussolini's foreign and imperial policy?

Mussolini: an assessment

The Rise to Power
Mussolini rose to power by exploiting Italy's political, social and economic crisis after the First World War to become Italy's youngest Prime Minister. Through a mixture of parliamentary campaigning and the use of violence, Mussolini turned his position as head of a right-wing coalition government into a personal dictatorship. Mussolini claimed he had risen to power as a result of the fear of communism. In reality, the Socialist Party's withdrawal from parliament following the Matteottti Affair allowed Mussolini to create the conditions for his dictatorship.

A Totalitarian Dictatorship?
Mussolini's regime was the least repressive of the inter-war dictators. Important institutions – the Catholic Church and Big Business – remained outside his immediate control and, although he effectively used propaganda to perpetrate the myth of the all-knowing, dynamic *Duce*, behind the political spin the Fascist regime faced ever growing problems during the 1930s. Italy was not prepared to meet the economic problems created by the Depression, and as Europe entered the Second World War Italy was almost completely unprepared. Mussolini was a weak dictator because Italy was weak. His position within both the Fascist Party and Italy deteriorated rapidly from 1942 with the collapse of the Italian military effort. Mussolini was peacefully overthrown by a coup within the Fascist Party and armed forces. His Social Republic of Salo was an independent political entity in name only. From 1943 to 1945 he was merely a puppet of Nazi Germany.

Foreign and Imperial Affairs
During his regime Mussolini was an internationally dominant figure. His ability to exploit international matters for his own benefit was a feature of his foreign policy. Throughout his career, both domestically and abroad, Mussolini was the archetypal opportunist. His conduct of foreign and imperial affairs can be divided into two phases: from 1922 to the early 1930s Mussolini displayed modest, traditional aims to increase Italy's international prestige; from the early 1930s his policies became increasingly aggressive. The Ethiopian war marked this turning point. However, from 1936 Mussolini, who once saw himself as arbiter of Europe, increasingly sided with Hitler. The decision to go to war in June 1940 on Hitler's side proved to be disastrous for Mussolini and Italy.

Mussolini's Legacy
When Mussolini died he was the most hated man in Italy. Following his death, anti-Fascism became a dominant force in Italian politics. From 1946, Italy voted to become a republic. Although a neo-Fascist Party did appear, it never went beyond the role of a fringe party. In reality, Fascism was unique to Italy and uniquely linked to the views and personality of Mussolini. Today 'fascism' is a term of abuse implying intolerance.

Further reading

Texts specifically designed for students

Blinkhorn. M, *Mussolini and Fascist Italy* (Routledge Lancaster Pamphlets, 1984)

Morris, T. and Murphy D, *Europe 1870–1991 (second edition)* (Collins, 2004)

Neville, P. *Mussolini* (Routledge, 2004)

Robson, M. *Italy: Liberalism and Fascism 1870–1945* (Hodder, 1992)

Townley, E. *Mussolini and Italy* (Heinemann, 2002)

Texts for more advanced study

Bosworth, R. J. B., *Mussolini* (Arnold, 2002) is a detailed political biography by Australia's leading authority on Mussolini and Fascist Italy. At 590 pages, Bosworth offers an interpretation of Mussolini which postdates Renzo de Felice's mammoth study of *Il Duce*. He reinterprets De Felice's views, ultimately regarding Mussolini's rule as a failure.

Deakin, F. W. *The Brutal Friendship, Mussolini, Hitler and the fall of Fascism* (Penguin, 1966) reappraises the early work on the Hitler-Mussolini relationship.

De Grand, A. *Italian Fascism*, second edition (University of Nebraska, 1989) is a short but advanced explanation of the main features of Fascism, including its origins and variety.

Finer, H. *Mussolini's Italy* (Victor Gollanz, 1935) is an interesting contemporary study of Mussolini from a left wing perspective. Published before the Italian invasion of Ethiopia. He sees Fascism as transient dependent exclusively on the talent of Mussolini.

Mack Smith, D. *Mussolini* (Weidenfeld and Nicolson, 1981) is a highly readable biography by Britain's foremost expert on Mussolini. It is a political biography in which Mack Smith portrays Mussolini as an opportunist in his quest for political power.

Mallett, R. *Mussolini and the Origins of the Second World War* (Macmillan, 2003) is the most up-to-date study of Mussolini's foreign policy in the lead up to the Second World War, in particular Mussolini's relationship with Hitler and Nazi Germany.

Index

Historians

Profiles

Main Index